SAILING
AN ATLANTIC
CIRCUIT

SAILING
AN ATLANTIC
CIRCUIT

ALASTAIR BUCHAN

ADLARD COLES NAUTICAL
London

Published 2002 by Adlard Coles Nautical
an imprint of A & C Black (Publishers) Ltd
37 Soho Square, London W1D 3QZ
www.adlardcoles.com

ISBN 0-7136-5998-X

A CIP catalogue record for this book is available from the British
Library.

Note: while all reasonable care has been taken in the publication of
this book, the publisher takes no responsibility for the use of the
methods or products described in the book.

Designed by Eric Drewery
Typeset in 10/12pt Galliard
Printed and bound in Great Britain
by Cromwell Press, Trowbridge, Wiltshire

Contents

10 The Eastward Crossing   120

11 Swallowing the Anchor   135

Introduction

Whilst I prepared *Mintaka* for my first passage to the Caribbean, other sailors in a thousand harbours, anchorages, marinas and boatyards scattered across Europe and America were also readying their boats to cross the Atlantic. I knew that I was not the first but I never realised that I was to be part of an international mob making its annual migration south. Nor did it occur to me that we would meet in every port and anchorage I visited and become part of a nautical touring community.

Every spring, dreamers of all nationalities raise their sails, sniff the air, turn towards the sun and head south, their tracks merging and crossing and merging again. Those who sail down-Channel from Denmark, Germany, Holland and France tend to gather in Falmouth waiting for a weather window for the jump to La Coruña, another great cruising village. Boats from Norway, Sweden, Finland and Poland have the choice of sailing round the top of Scotland or dropping through the Caledonian Canal before heading for Southern Ireland and on to La Coruña. Then there are homeward bound American, Canadian, Australian and New Zealand yachts who, unlike their European cousins, began not with familiar coastal passages but were immediately faced with ocean passages! To us novice dreamers they are the experts on blue-water sailing.

As the coast slips away and the miles mount under our keels, nationality becomes irrelevant. We are all members of the blue-water cruising tribe, known by our boat's name, not its flag, and membership is sufficient introduction to discuss plans, to swap information and to seek and offer help.

I planned to make no more than one passage across the Atlantic and another back, a solitary crossing the ocean for its own satisfaction, made in my own yacht, *Mintaka*, a simple ambition shared by thousands of yachtsmen and women. What evolved was a circular cruise with friends that I could join wherever it suited, stay with as long as I liked, go where I wanted and visit any island, port, or anchorage that took my fancy. I sailed at my own pace, stopped for as long as I liked whenever I wished. It was a magic time. I enjoyed it so much that within two years I had sold *Mintaka*, bought and refitted *Margo* and started out again.

Both cruises were a steep learning curve. I have tried in this book to include all the information, hints and tips I would like to have known before I sailed. I do not expect everyone to agree with everything I say (no one ever has) but I hope that this book will give you some useful advice based on practical experience that will help to see you safely and happily across the Atlantic. May you learn from my mistakes.

1 The Dreamer's Charter

I had barely cleared the marina's lock gates when a sneak attack of rain wiped out Hartlepool. The town vanished behind a veil of grey leaving *Mintaka* alone on a sorrowing sea. This was not in my script or, for that matter, the day's weather forecast. The plot called for blue skies, sparkling seas and the massed paraphernalia of the media recording the cheering throng while I played the modest, but handsome, hero of the hour. I was setting out single-handed to cross the Atlantic and live the dream but the reality was so miserable and depressing that if I could have found a decent excuse amongst the chaos of the forepeak I would have called the whole thing off and gone home.

Like most yachtsmen with a bent towards cruising I dreamt of sailing in warm seas and amenable winds but prior engagements and pressing commitments always stood in the way. For years my dreams had been little more than a comfort blanket to snuggle under when reading accounts of far flung cruises. I acquired the bedrock for a fine stock of armchair opinions bolstered by second-hand knowledge but deep down I knew that if I really wanted to, I could sail the ocean blue and I had the jargon to prove it.

An ocean of dreams and siren songs, the Atlantic finds new challenges for each generation. Long before Columbus arrived in the Bahamas seamen from Phoenicia, Wales, Ireland, Norway and Portugal, the English West Country and Galicia had ventured west. Some claimed to have found new lands. The Vikings pioneered the cold northern route and by AD 1000 established settlements as far south as L'Anse aux Meadows in Newfoundland where they left evidence of voyages still further south. By August 1492 when Columbus left Pálos de La Frontera in southern Spain, a fair-sized body of knowledge existed on what the ancients called the Sea of Darkness, and according to one legend Columbus used a well-thumbed copy of the second edition of the Atlantic Pilot to light his way across.

Today, the challenge of sailing across the Atlantic is not one of exploration, or proving a particular vessel can cross, or record breaking, or claiming a 'first'. It has all been long done. Today's challenge is personal. It asks if you have what it takes to cross the Atlantic and the first step in the journey to find an answer is to leave the pontoon.

One day I heard a voice declaring that it liked the idea of cruising in the direction of the West Indies. Another silly fool, I thought and then realised that I had opened my big mouth once too often. Fortunately, only my wife, Liz, was there to witness this ridiculous outburst but instead of laughing it to scorn as any sensible spouse ought she treated the whole idea as though it was nothing more than a day-sail writ large. Taken aback, I hurriedly pointed out that I would be away for a year or more. There were no hoots of derision and having pushed the boat out I had to work out how to get it to the other side. Like charity, losing face begins at home.

It is one thing to prop up the yacht club bar and talk knowledgeably about crossing the Atlantic. Giving ambition a voice moves reality to a newer, higher level. If there was a time to quit then it was before any commitment was made and that depended upon my answers to three questions:

First, could I cross the Atlantic in *Mintaka*?

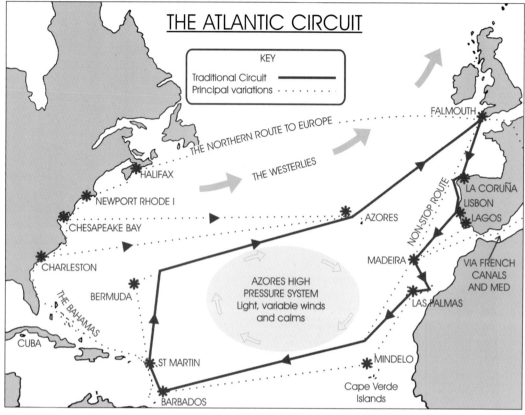

THE ATLANTIC CIRCUIT

KEY
Traditional Circuit ——————
Principal variations · · · · · · · ·

FALMOUTH
THE NORTHERN ROUTE TO EUROPE
HALIFAX
THE WESTERLIES
NEWPORT RHODE I
LA CORUÑA
LISBON
CHESAPEAKE BAY
AZORES
LAGOS
NON-STOP ROUTE
CHARLESTON
MADEIRA
VIA FRENCH
CANALS
AND MED
AZORES HIGH
PRESSURE SYSTEM
Light, variable winds
and calms
BERMUDA
THE BAHAMAS
LAS PALMAS
CUBA
ST MARTIN
MINDELO
Cape Verde
Islands
BARBADOS

Fig 1 *The traditional Atlantic Circuit and principal variations.*

She is a twin-keeled, Hurley 20, well-equipped but still only 20 feet LOA.

Second, how long would it take? I could reel off crossing times like football scores but how long would I take to sail across the Atlantic and back? Most published figures are for one-way passages. A year for a round trip seemed a reasonable guess but was it right and would it be fair on Liz to stay away so long? Thirdly, could the family piggy bank stand the strain? Three very simple questions but if the answer to any one of them was 'No' then all bets were off and I would return to the pontoon eating my humble pie.

THE PRICE OF EVERYTHING

My last question was, 'Can I afford it?' There is little point preparing for an Atlantic Circuit only to run out of money before you sail but it is difficult to figure out the costs. I tried writing lists of work and equipment and placing estimated costs against each item. When I added my figures up I discovered that I planned to spend money in quantities that would have shocked my Aberdonian grandfather. It was very close to a 'No'.

Non-recoverable capital costs head any list. Their scale depends partly on your boat and partly on how much work you decide is necessary to make your yacht ready. Small is now beautiful: buying a winch or a new sail for a 20-foot yacht may hurt but not as much as buying one for a 32-foot yacht. Before I sailed in 1996 I spent almost £4000, with over half going on safety equipment. This worked out at about a third of the total costs and this ratio held true for most folk I met on the way round.

It is a delusion that capital expenditure is recoverable. The shiny new equipment you buy for the trip adds little to the value of your yacht. It might just be possible to recover some

THE PIONEERS

I know that most folk reckon that a Hurley 20 is rather small to sail across the Atlantic and that twin-keeled yachts are considered unsuitable for ocean passages – two strikes against me before I had even begun but this was not a democracy and I was not taking a vote. I was in the fortunate position of having no one to convince but myself. *Mintaka* and I had crossed the North Sea several times and sailed round Britain together. It added up to a lot of sea miles and not always in fair weather. Surely that counted for something? Also, I had a vague recollection that yachts of 25 feet LOA and less had pioneered crossing the Atlantic for fun.

Wrong. The first yacht to cross the Atlantic was the 83-foot *Cleopatra's Barge* sailing from west to east in 1817. It was a mega-yacht of its day and ended its time as a commercial packet ship. In 1856 the 43-foot *Charter Oak*, similar in size to many modern blue-water cruisers, sailed from America to Europe.

The first small yacht to attempt the passage was the 24-foot *Vision*. She sailed on 24 June 1864 bound for Europe. Given three masts and rigged as a brigantine with three square sails on the foremast (!) she had a crew of three including a dog. But apart from a brief sighting two days out from New York the *Vision* was never heard of again.

Two years later the 26-foot *Red White and Blue*, a prototype lifeboat built in galvanised steel, sailed from New York on 9 July 1866 and arrived in Deal, Kent 35 days later. A very respectable performance, for like the *Vision*, she too had three masts and was square-rigged on all three. A square sail has much to commend itself for a trade wind passage but on a west-to-east passage, square sails on a small yacht must have been a sore trial.

But she showed that small boats could cross the Atlantic safely and thereafter one or two crept across each year, mostly from America to Europe. In 1870 the 20-foot *City of Ragusa* with a crew of two plus a dog became the first small yacht to cross from east to west and then sailed back to Europe to complete the first small-ship Atlantic Circuit. Six years later the 20-foot *Centennial* made the first single-handed passage. Great, all I had to do was combine these two voyages. As an extra reassurance my list of small boat crossings flourished. Small yachts, canoes, inflatables (including RIBs), rafts, rowing boats, pedal boats, windsurfers and a jeep have all made it across.

There is a fine distinction between making a seamanlike crossing in a small yacht, and putting to sea in a freak craft. Where this line is drawn is a matter of individual judgement. Is a yacht under 15–16 foot LOA freakish? Perhaps, but it is imprudent to be dogmatic. Robert Manry who crossed in the 13-foot *Tinkerbelle* in 1965, or Gerry Spiess in his 10-foot *Yankee Girl* in 1979, or Tom McClean in the 9-foot 9-inch *Giltspur* and 9-foot *Will's Way* are examples to us all and a reminder that seamanship and seaworthiness are not in direct proportion to overall length.

The pioneers made their voyages in the days of wooden ships, canvas sails, and hemp ropes. By modern standards their vessels were ill-equipped. Slocum did not have a stove until he reached Gibraltar. *Mintaka* not only had a stove she had roller-reefing headsails, self-steering, GPS, and radios. No doubt I would add more gear before I left. Almost without realising it I decided *Mintaka* had what it takes to cross the Atlantic.

money on your return by selling individual items such as wind generators, self-steering units and HF radios but this should not be relied upon. Sailing equipment, especially electronics, dates quickly and becomes almost worthless when you are the seller rather than the buyer. The only sure way to reduce capital costs is to delete items from the list.

Other cash paid out or laid aside before you sail includes the emergency fund and insurance premiums. The emergency fund is money you must find very quickly to meet any demand for instant funds. At the very least this should cover the price of tickets for flying the entire crew home. With luck this money will be spent celebrating your return as planned.

Insurance premiums split into boat insurance and personal insurance. Boat insurance for ocean passages is not cheap but the good news is that you are really only paying the difference between your normal cruising range and ocean cruising. Over the years my insurance company had been tolerant of my wanderings. I would telephone

them from foreign parts, and ask to extend my cruising range and for a small fee they agreed. On this occasion I thought it would be best to telephone them before I arrived in the Caribbean. The lass in their office expressed no surprise that I was going to the Caribbean. She had only two questions. 'Will you confirm that *Mintaka* is 20 LOA?' I did and she enquired 'Are you intending to take *Mintaka* to the Caribbean by road or ferry?' It was the end of a beautiful relationship.

For blue-water passages, insurers frequently impose restrictions or insist that certain, expensive equipment is on board. They may only offer cover for vessels above a certain size or value. They may insist on a minimum crew size. Three is a popular number. They will almost certainly exclude cruising in hurricane areas during the hurricane season. Accept their conditions and they are likely to ask for a much higher deductible (excess) of over £1000. If you find comprehensive cover too expensive, consider taking out third party cover for the entire voyage and arrange separate cover for coastal and immediate offshore areas. Ocean passages are then at your own risk but when you arrive in Spain, the Canaries or the Caribbean you will be insured.

Anything not bolted to the deck or hull is normally defined as personal belongings and equipment, and usually excluded from marine insurance policies. On a long cruise you carry far more personal belongings than usual so check this point out, and if necessary take out a separate personal insurance policy.

Annual Personal Costs

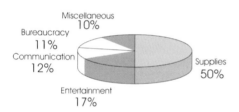

Annual Boat Costs

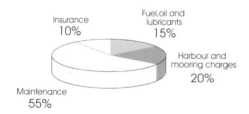

Atlantic Circuit Costs

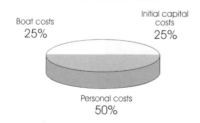

Fig 2 *Pie charts showing annual personal costs, annual boat costs and costs for the actual circuit.*

PERSONAL COSTS

How much you spend on day-to-day living depends on how high on the hog you choose to live. If you insist on gourmet dinners then your figure will be fatter and your costs higher than those who boil rice and open a can of tuna. If, in port, you eat in the best restaurants, hire cars and take every sightseeing trip as though on a two-week package holiday then costs will be high.

For shore transport as far as the Canaries, a folding cycle beats walking and is cheaper than taxis. In the Caribbean, road conditions, longer distances and a good cheap public transport network make cycling more demanding and less attractive.

For me an unforeseen extra was paying to enter, and sometimes to leave, Caribbean countries. Most of these countries charge a fee for each crew member, and for issuing a cruising permit. Some demand that you have a visa and a few occasionally arrange matters so that you pay overtime charges when you check in or out. Although most yachts rarely enter a harbour and navigation lights throughout the Caribbean are spectacularly unreliable, it is usual to pay harbour and lights dues. The average cost of clearing into each country is between $25–100, more if you have a large crew. There are over 30 countries in the Caribbean Basin.

BOAT COSTS

Boat costs include the obvious like fuel, oil and lubricants. The near absence of berthing charges comes as a pleasant surprise. Staying in marinas is a bad habit but once away from European waters, anchoring is the rule, and for the most part free. For those who cannot break the habit there are marinas. Prices vary from 50 cents a foot per night to around $4 per foot per night with power extra and cable TV adding around 10% to the bill for a 38-foot yacht. In the Caribbean, water is also extra and in some marinas, water charges based on LOA are added automatically to the price whether you use their water or not. Without power, TV or water charges and based on a totally unrepresentative sample, the average charge for a 38-foot yacht is probably between $1.25–1.50 per foot per night, say $50–60 (£30–40) per night and there may well be local taxes on top of these figures. For a short summer cruise these costs are bearable but over a year or more they will devour your budget.

Discounts are available for longer stays but at the height of the sailing season, when marinas are at their busiest, their charges reflect the increased demand and boats frequently book ahead days or weeks in advance. This is particularly true if a recent hurricane has damaged marinas and taken berths out of use. This is also the time when staying in marinas means living with the hassle of rebuilding work. In the Virgin Islands there is also a practice of laying moorings in the more popular anchorages. Anchoring is almost impossible and charges for using a mooring are close to those of a marina berth.

Maintenance is not a feature of the usual three-week summer cruise so the higher than expected maintenance charges hurt. They were incurred not because *Mintaka* or *Margo* was falling apart but rather because living aboard encourages constant daily maintenance. Everybody was always working on their boat. Then there are unmissable bargains or that item of equipment you must have. One way or another it adds up to between 40–50% of your day-to-day budget.

Faced with a long list of unknowns and wild guesstimates I decided to reverse-engineer my day-to-day budget. I came up with a weekly figure I could afford and resolved to stick to it. For a variety of reasons this was not always possible: when provisioning for a long passage there is a tendency to buy more than I will ever eat, and a few days partying or two or three side trips to see the world make a mockery of any budget, but at least I knew when I was being extravagant and, in the end, the figure I used was not wildly adrift.

Creative accounting deluded me into believing that the figures were reasonable. Ashore or afloat I would still have to pay out day-to-day living costs and if I included my annual marina fee, insurance costs, lift out charges, annual refit expenses and the usual season's fuel budget I had a respectable figure to set against my cruising budget to make it look affordable.

If you have a car laid up for the duration of your cruise then its running costs can be set against the day-to-day costs and if you are leaving a house or a flat unoccupied while you are sailing for a year or more, then a popular way of raising some income to offset day-to-day costs is to rent it out.

You might even show a profit if you have a crew of friends (as opposed to family) for the costs of provisioning, harbour dues and entry fees can be shared. Be warned that most insurance policies exclude commercial operations and it may be prudent to check with your insurance company where they draw the line between friends sharing costs and paying passengers.

No two boats will have the same budget. Amongst variables to be taken into account are:

- Lifestyle and personal circumstances
- DIY skills to keep maintenance costs down
- Number in crew
- Size and type of vessel

How you factor these points into your equations will determine your final budget.

TIMINGS

My third and last question was when should I sail and how long would I be away?

Pioneers often sailed at unusual times of the year. In 1577 when he left Plymouth on his circumnavigation Drake sailed on 15 November and ran into a gale that blew one ship ashore and dismasted his ship. Three centuries later the first transatlantic race between the *Henrietta*, *Vesta* and *Fleetwing* was held in December 1866. Departures often took place in late June and July when there was (and is) a real, though small, risk of meeting a hurricane. In his book *Half Safe* Ben Carlin describes being caught in a tropical storm between the Azores and Madeira in December 1950. The Carlins had left Halifax late in July. David Johnstone and John Hoare in the rowing dory *Puffin* were lost in Hurricane Faith some time in September 1966 as they raced Ridgway and Blyth across the Atlantic. They had left Virginia Beach, Norfolk on 21 May. In the last week of June 1968 entrants in the Single-Handed Transatlantic Race from Plymouth to Newport RI were heading towards Hurricane Brenda (the second of the season!)

Timings for an Atlantic Loop

Action	J	F	M	A	M	J	J	A	S	O	N	D	J	F	M	A	M	J	J	A	S	O	N	D
Refit: Probably begun previous Oct/Nov	█	█	█	█	█	█	█																	
Outward Cruise: British & N.European Coasts					▒	▒																		
Passage to North West Spain						▓	▓																	
Cruise Northern Spanish & Portuguese Coasts							▒	▒																
Passage to Madeiras: boats from Med join here								▓	▓															
Cruise Madeira									▒															
Passage to the Canaries									▓	▓														
Cruise the Canaries										▒														
Passage to the Caribbean											░	░												
Cruise the Caribbean inc Bahamas & E Coast USA												▒	▒	▒	▒	▒								
Passage to the Azores																		░	░					
Cruise Azores																			▒	▒				
Passage to British & N.European Coasts																				▓	▓			
Homeward Cruise: British & N.European Coasts																					▒	▒		
HURRICANE SEASON																		▒	▒	▒	▒	▒	▒	

KEY	
Shorebased activities	█
Day sailing	▒
Passages under 1000nm	▓
Passages over 1000nm	░

NOTE: It is possible to cruise the Madeiras and the Canaries all year round. With care or by sailing south out of the hurricane zone it is possible to sail all year round in the Caribbean.

which was travelling east more or less along the latitude of the Azores.

Why sail when there is a risk of hurricanes? Was I missing something? Re-reading accounts of transatlantic passages, one factor stood out. Those who sailed late in the season had met unforeseen problems and delays in their preparations, fallen far behind schedule and faced the choice of sailing much later than planned or quitting. Those who sail the Atlantic are not quitters. For me the lesson was clear. Double the time for preparations and then add half as much again as a cushion against unexpected problems.

Even then be wary of a firm commitment to leave on a particular day. It concentrates the mind but it can be a rod for your own back. If a few days' delay would see the forepeak decently stowed, last-minute stores delivered and vital work properly completed and tested then it is time well lost.

Donald Crowhurst on *Teignmouth Electron* was caught both ways in this trap. He had too little time for preparation and a firmly fixed departure date. Committed emotionally, financially and publicly he started the 1968 Golden Globe Round the World Race with his boat unfinished, gear unstowed and generally unready to sail. It is impossible to avoid speculating what part this hasty start played in the subsequent tragedy.

Good weather can never be guaranteed, especially at the margins of a season. I decided to aim for the middle of each weather window where comfort and lazy sailing is most likely to be found. This also provided a start date easily varied, a euphemism for 'delayed', without cutting it too fine, although in *Margo* I managed to come close.

Unless taking to the French canals it is best to wait for the end of the spring gales before crossing the Bay of Biscay. This window closes when the equinoctial gales blow in from the Atlantic when, if you want fair weather, you ought to be somewhere close to Madeira or the Azores. Both Madeira, which the square-riggers called 'the Island', and the Azores are a two to three weeks' sail from the European mainland; if you decide to sail direct to them from Europe it places the latest sensible departure in the middle of August.

Once in the Canaries the next weather window opens at the end of November with the closing performances of the hurricane season. This is the earliest reasonable time for leaving the Canaries for the Caribbean although other factors come into play. Boats in the Atlantic Rally for Cruisers (ARC) leave Las Palmas on the last Sunday in November so as to have a fair chance of arriving in St Lucia in time to join the Christmas parties. It is still possible to spend Christmas in the Canaries and still have time to sail to the Caribbean, or sail south in December to the Cape Verde Islands; or spend Christmas a few miles further south in Dakar.

Most yachts arrive in the Caribbean in late December or early January. This gives five months of warm, blue-water cruising before the next hurricane season. If the plan includes returning to Europe it is necessary to be at a suitable departure port in the Caribbean or the eastern seaboard of the USA and sail clear of the hurricane zone before the season's first storm arrives. A useful rule of thumb is to be in the Azores before the end of June. This leaves a few weeks to explore the Azores before sailing back to Europe in time to avoid the start of the autumn gales, and working backwards, it means leaving the USA or the Caribbean around the middle of May.

If you decide to remain in the Caribbean then during late April or early May you should implement your chosen hurricane season strategy.

It all adds up to a programme stretching over a year to fifteen months with another six to nine months spent refitting before setting out – say two years in total. Corners can and are cut. Refitting time pruned to three or four months, and it is possible to leave in April, sail to the Caribbean, turn round and sail straight back home again to arrive in August (it has been done) but this is a lot of sailing for very little fun.

I found the planning and preparation phases the loneliest of times. My knowledge and understanding of what I was attempting was entirely theoretical or second-hand and much of what I read stressed bad weather, danger and hardships, all of which I find unattractive. I was also extrapolating coastal and offshore experience further than common sense suggested. As a result I was beset by doubts and unanswered questions and there was no one I could turn to for reassurance. It would have been easy to give up.

From the top of Scandinavia throughout the length of Europe to the foot of Italy and along the eastern seaboard of the USA, folk were struggling to find their own answers to the same questions, facing the same dilemmas and suffering the same highs and lows. They were reading the same books, searching the same catalogues, counting their pennies and doing the same sums. For some, years of work and preparation were coming to an end.

Others, like me, were jumping in with both feet. There are associations like the OCC (Ocean Cruising Club) for those who have made an ocean passage but there is no club for potential ocean cruisers. At this stage we are isolated, solitary dreamers but soon our tracks would come together and join those of the great and good tribe of blue-water cruisers where finding advice and support is no problem. But that was the future. Just now it was solitary hard work with little obvious reward.

I explained my timings and concerns to Liz who did not quibble at seeing the back of me for over a year and scorned my doubts. Three questions, three positive answers, all I had to do now was prepare *Mintaka* for the trip of her life.

. . . And suddenly nearing Faial I was not alone.

2 Preparing Your Boat

Proper preparation is crucial to any project, but refitting for a year-long cruise is as much a journey into the unknown as crossing an ocean. The Atlantic Circuit involves sailing 10,000 miles in 15 months, about the same distance most yachtsmen sail in 10 to 15 years of normal cruising. How do you prepare a yacht for 10 years' wear and tear in a single year?

THE IDEAL BOAT

The lazy man's refit is to buy the ideal boat. With luck, most of the cost would be recouped by selling it on your return. However, what makes the ideal blue-water cruising yacht is a debate without an end. If the yardstick is 'Can it cross an ocean?' then yachts of all sizes, hull shapes, and rigs meet it. They have been built of wood, GRP, concrete, steel, aluminium, canvas and rubber. Once, Bernard Moitessier contemplated building a boat out of paper and sailing it back to France. There have been big yachts and small yachts, yachts with single chine hulls, multi-chine hulls, and round hulls, mono-hulls, and of course, multihulls. The first multihull to cross the Atlantic was the 42-foot *Ananda* that sailed from France to Martinique in 1947. They have been rigged as sloops, cutters, ketches, schooners, brigantines, and ships. They have been powered by Bermudan rigs, gaff rigs, freedom rigs, junk rigs, kites and rigid-computer-controlled wing sails. They have had aft cockpits, centre cockpits, and in the case of yachts like *Jester*, no cockpit. They have had full keels, fin keels, lifting keels, wing keels and twin keels. They have been given diesel engines, petrol engines, outboard engines and no engine. The list includes production boats, one-off designs and 'innovative' designs as well as new boats, old boats, home built boats, and conversions too modest to mention their age or antecedents.

This is not culled from reference books. Visit the Muelle Deportivo in Las Palmas in the Canaries around November and you will see various permutations of all these types making ready to cross the Atlantic. Every owner believes their craft is ideal and they have all sailed well over a thousand miles off soundings to prove it. It would be silly to claim one type of vessel or design, method of construction, hull form or building material is better suited than another. Some boats may sail faster, others may be more comfortable but all will make the voyage.

SPACE BELOW DECKS

Bear in mind that for a year or more the boat will be your home. Small yachts lack standing headroom. Once in the tropics where the cockpit is the principal living area this is not much of a problem but sitting headroom only is usually associated with a lack of living space below decks and a lifestyle on passage resembling the squalid conditions of a small, wet, mountain tent.

Everyone aboard needs one space below deck to call their own. Hot bunking is out, so too is a saloon that spends half its life pretending to be a bedroom. Size is dictated more by the number in the crew than by performance with a marked preference for beamy yachts with a high internal volume. A typical 32-foot LOA cruising yacht with a nominal six berths will provide comfortable accommodation for two, three at a pinch and four if they are very good friends. The average size of yachts crossing the Atlantic has risen to 40–45 feet LOA: most have crews of three or four.

PERFORMANCE AND SAIL HANDLING

Windward performance is not a high priority. Most blue-water sailing is reaching or running. This makes a hull form with good lateral stability desirable. Given a preference for a high internal volume to maximise living space, it adds up to a broad-beamed bath-tub. Do not scoff. This is a fair description of Columbus' caravels and his best time for the crossing was 21 days. In 1573 on his voyage home from the Caribbean, Drake is supposed to have sailed back to Plymouth in 23 days.

An easily-handled rig is important. Best of all is a rig where you do not have to leave the cockpit to set or reef sails. Most headsails are fitted to some form of roller-reefing system with the control lines led back to the cockpit. Over the years, headsail roller-reefing systems have proved very reliable, though on the rare occasions when they do fail it is always spectacularly inconvenient.

Off the wind, ketches and schooners can throw up between-mast staysails, the lazy man's spinnaker, and romp away. Twin masts break the sail plan into small chunks managed easily by one person and for that reason are popular with blue-water cruisers, but modern sail-handling systems have eroded that advantage.

A mainsail that needs one person on the helm, and a second handling sails, places a considerable strain on the crew, especially during night watches where reefing means rousing someone from their bunk. In such cases, sail changes are often left to a change each watch, which still shortens someone's rest, or a reef is taken in before dark, regardless of wind conditions, which slows the boat down. Single-handed mainsail handling options include in-mast or in-boom reefing systems or single line slab reefing

systems with jackstays to catch the sail as it is lowered. All have their supporters and detractors, none are cheap and most require either modifying your existing mainsail or buying a new sail. Lateral solutions include opting for a junk rig or a wing sail.

THE BOAT YOU KNOW

It is possible that the perfect boat could be the one that you have now. You know its good and bad points and, just as important, it knows you. *Mintaka* had carried me safely for many thousands of miles and we had long since come to an understanding. She did the sailing and I did as I was told. I knew every creak and squeak she made, how close she would lie to the wind in different conditions, how much sail she would happily carry in any given wind strength and sea state. She had her faults. A short waterline meant that she would never be fast and the outboard hanging from her stern gave a limited range under power and was near useless in anything above a calm, and going upwind in winds above a force five was a delusion, but we had faith in each other.

REFITTING AND MODIFICATIONS

Over the years many small modifications had made *Mintaka* more suitable for my type of sailing. There had never been a major refit, just one or two small improvements each winter lay-up. Those that had not worked had either been re-thought and redone or ripped out. By the time I came to cross the Atlantic, a huge amount of work had been done, tried and tested but always in small increments. If this is the case with you, think long and hard before investing in a new boat. Whether brand-new or second-hand and new to you, a huge amount of work will be needed before you are happy with it.

A reasonably thorough inspection will produce a list of tasks longer than expected and as work progresses, unforeseen defects and deficiencies will be discovered. Nor is

Above: Mintaka *is a twin-keeled Hurley 20, sloop-rigged. A diminutive boat for an Atlantic crossing, but she was a boat I knew well and trusted.*
Below: I resolved to have a boat which gave me room to stand up below and provide me with a few more creature comforts; Margo *is a shoal-draft Dockerell 27 with cutter rig.*

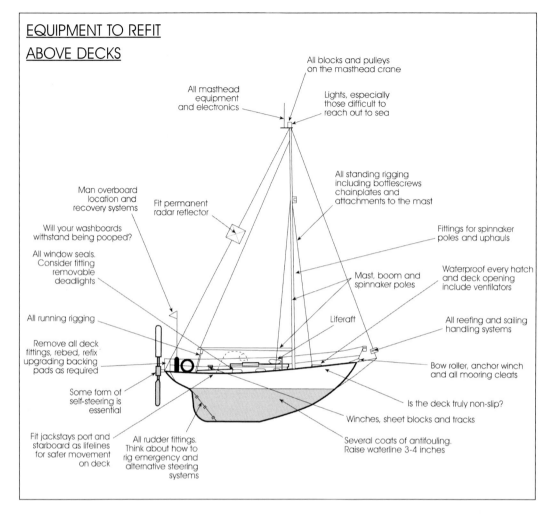

EQUIPMENT TO REFIT
ABOVE DECKS

All blocks and pulleys
on the masthead crane

All masthead
equipment
and electronics

Lights, especially
those difficult to
reach out to sea

All standing rigging
including bottlescrews
chainplates and
attachments to the mast

Man overboard
location and
recovery systems

Fit permanent
radar reflector

Will your washboards
withstand being pooped?

Fittings for spinnaker
poles and uphauls

All window seals.
Consider fitting
removable
deadlights

Mast, boom and
spinnaker poles

Waterproof every hatch
and deck opening
include ventilators

All running rigging

Liferaft

All reefing and sailing
handling systems

Remove all deck
fittings, rebed, refix
upgrading backing
pads as required

Bow roller, anchor winch
and all mooring cleats

Some form of
self-steering is
essential

Is the deck truly non-slip?

Winches, sheet blocks and tracks

Fit jackstays port and
starboard as lifelines
for safer movement
on deck

All rudder fittings.
Think about how to
rig emergency and
alternative steering
systems

Several coats of antifouling.
Raise waterline 3-4 inches

Fig 3 *Rigging and essential equipment above decks.*

work limited to straightforward replacement and upgrading. It is almost certain that a number of modifications will recommend themselves to you. They may seem desirable, even sensible, but you will not know how they will work until you take them to sea and if experience proves them unsuitable then time for remedial work is limited.

I learnt this the hard way on *Margo*. After nearly two years of cramped, sitting headroom, I resolved to have a boat that I could stand up in when I went below. The ability to stand erect in the cabin would, so I reasoned, provide more than enough gracious living space for my needs and vastly

improve my comfort factor. *Margo* is a Dockerell 27, which means she is a shoal draft, cutter-rigged version of the Hurley 27 or a bigger version of *Mintaka*. I bought her one spring, and spent the summer sailing and planning the winter refit. The intention was to finish this by April, spend a month in sea trials, another month for any remedial work and then, in July, make a gentle voyage to Falmouth. The reality saw *Margo* launched in mid-August; a hurried passage to Falmouth passed for sea trials. Consequently I found that there were problem areas, like the galley, and I spent two years wishing I had allowed more time for the refit.

A good refitting programme falls into two phases: servicing the existing fittings and equipment and then making modifications. The division is not clear-cut but it is useful for planning purposes and at the top of the list is to keep the sea out and the cabin dry.

KEEPING THE SEA OUT

The amount of water crossing the deck in heavy weather, off soundings, is unbelievable: every hole in the hull and deck is a potential leak. None are likely to be life-threatening but all carry the certain promise of misery. Every single deck fitting on both *Mintaka* and *Margo* was removed, checked, bedded down on the best sealant I could find and refitted. This is a huge task and includes the stem-head fitting (bow roller), chainplates, stanchion bases, cleats, jammers, winches, windlasses, hawse pipes, grabrails, harness anchor points, tabernacles and mast fittings, hatches and windows.

When a yacht is built, many deck fittings are installed before the hull and deck are put together. Afterwards they can be removed only by professional contortionists. Sometimes a layer or two of chopped strand mat, laid over a nut, passes for 'encapsulating', but its primary purpose is to make it impossible to fit a spanner over the nut, and the faith some boat builders have in penny or even halfpenny washers as backing pads to strong points is little short of astounding.

LEAKING HATCHES

Despite annual applications of neoprene tape, *Mintaka*'s forehatch leaked, not badly, but in rough weather there was a steady drip that soaked the forepeak. Several tubes of sealant made it absolutely watertight but unless I dug out the sealant, the hatch was permanently closed. This gave rise to the criticism that in an emergency I could not escape through the forehatch, a fair point, but I could hardly climb out of the forehatch even when I could open it.

For the mainhatch, *Mintaka* and *Margo*

both had washboards of $\frac{1}{2}$in (12 mm) plywood dropped into a length of rebated wood fastened to the side of the hatchway by brass screws. I had visions of sitting in the cabin, holding the washboards and wondering why I was knee deep in water. This is a common arrangement for holding washboards in place and the easy solution is to bolt a strip of $\frac{3}{4}$in (5mm) stainless steel to the inside of the hatchway. A more elaborate but stronger answer is to make new runners out of stainless steel that bolt to the front of the hatchway.

The hatches to cockpit lockers and lazarettes should be capable of being fastened shut and have seals. Self-adhesive neoprene tape makes good seals.

Margo has a hatch in the cockpit floor opening onto the engine space. It gives excellent access when working on the engine but it was held on by two hinges on its forward edge and secured by a hasp and staple aft. Without a padlock, the hasp and staple was useless and I discovered that the hinges were held to the cockpit by self-tapping screws into GRP. Imagine that hatch popping open in a seaway and being pooped. I did – and made arrangements for it to be bolted down.

If there is a hatch you do not need, then think about sealing it down permanently. Otherwise check its seals and replace any that are suspect. If possible, install fittings for strongbacks so that in heavy weather the chance of a hatch being forced open by a sea is much reduced.

DECKHOUSE WINDOWS

After hatches, windows are the biggest holes in the deck and hull. Some window frames have rubber or plastic seals in metal frames. Unless the seals are new, they should be replaced, for the tropical sun shortens their life dramatically. The seals and fastening mechanism of any opening windows, especially inward-opening windows, should be checked very carefully; if there is any doubt about their integrity they should be replaced.

The windows on some yachts are Perspex

bolted over holes cut in the sides of the coachroof. In some cases self-tapping screws are used instead of bolts to hold the windows in place. I am sure this is good practice but I prefer bolts. Given a decent thickness of Perspex and a liberal application of sealant this produces a strong and secure window but in the sun Perspex becomes brittle and should be replaced every two or three years. This is not a difficult task but Perspex does not like being cut or drilled. All can go well until the last inch is sawn or the final hole is drilled when there is a crack and the sheet splits from side to side. The answer, and it does not always work, is to use sharp tools; saw slowly to keep the blade cool and, wherever possible, to drill holes slowly using a bench drill.

It is tempting to replace Perspex windows with a polycarbonate like Lexan. This is much friendlier to work and far less likely to split but, despite claims to be resistant to ultra-violet, I have found polycarbonate windows going smoky in the sun.

If it is possible for a wave to push the windows into the cabin then consider fitting storm boards. These are wooden boards, of at least half-inch plywood, that are bolted over the outside of the windows to protect them from seas. One or two small 'portholes' cut in the board will allow light to enter the cabin.

Margo's 'roll bar' goes over the sprayhood and ties into the coachroof grabrails.

GRABRAILS

The traditional wooden grabrail running along the coachroof is usually held on by screws from the underside of the deck. I have never heard of a failure, and given the thickness of the wood, not sure that through-bolting would be stronger, but all grabrails should be removed, cleaned up, rebedded and refixed. If there is any doubt about their condition then they should be replaced.

As you leave the cockpit to go forward to work on deck it is instinctive to hang onto the pramhood. On *Margo* the pramhood has a framework of aluminium tubing held to the coachroof by a couple of small bolts. This is fine for holding up a pramhood but I had

visions of going over the side and taking the whole arrangement with me.

A stainless steel roll bar running over the top of the sprayhood made a splendid handhold and doubled as a boom crutch. To prevent it wobbling fore and aft it was necessary to have a support running forward on either side so the opportunity was taken to remove the wooden grabrails that ran along the top of the coachroof and use the supports of the roll bar as grabrails. In a further refinement these were placed higher than the original rails so that as I stepped out of the cockpit my hand would naturally drop onto them without having to bend down.

Since making the roll bar I have seen pramhoods using stainless steel tubing for the frame with cut outs in the canvas so the frame can be used as a handhold. This is a vast improvement on my aluminium tubing but if you opt for this then do check how it is fastened to the coachroof.

BOW ROLLERS

Long before I set off across the Atlantic I had fitted an improved bow roller to *Mintaka*. It would not have been out of place on a 35-foot yacht. When I looked at the mixture of aluminium and stainless steel that was *Margo*'s bow roller, and imagined anchor chain snatching at it in a blow, it had to go. At the very least it would leak. I should not have been surprised. Bow rollers on many production yachts are more ornamental than useful.

The off-the-shelf replacements were pretty-looking aluminium things that the forestay fitting would eat in a season's sailing. My answer was to make a new bow roller out of $\frac{3}{8}$in (5mm) stainless steel plate using 4in (10cm) diameter stainless steel rod for the rollers spinning round a 1in (25mm) pin. Pin diameter is important on anchor rollers: not only does it add strength but the greater its diameter, the easier it is for the rollers to rotate under load.

Metal working is beyond me and welding a mystery but when you want a one-off, tailor-made item it is usually possible to find a small machine shop that can do the work, provided you explain what is required without nautical jargon. Simple drawings, giving dimensions and mock-ups in plywood, are a tremendous help. Perhaps because this type of work is out of the ordinary run I have always found that these small workshops take great pains to produce a first class job. I usually supply the materials but if the scrap yard cannot help, the local metal suppliers can normally lay hands on what I need. Do not limit your search to specialist marine machine shops. Some of my best work was done by a firm that made stainless steel kitchens and the search for a means of bending stainless steel tube ended with a firm dealing in hydraulic supplies.

I replaced the original bow roller on Margo *with a substantial fitting made of stainless steel plate.*

STANDING AND RUNNING RIGGING

The standing and running rigging should be carefully checked. If the standing rigging is close to the end of its safe working life (about 8–10 years) then it and the bottlescrews (turnbuckles) ought to be replaced. This will be a major expense and the only comfort is that replacement now is cheaper than a broken mast later. When renewing the standing rigging, a few pennies more pays for upgrading to the next size of wire and buys extra peace of mind. If you are considering installing an HF marine radio then this is the time to fit the insulators to the backstay and, when your yacht is out of the water, is also the time to install a suitable ground plate for your HF radio.

When the mast is down, it is a good opportunity to replace the bulbs in spreader lights, steaming light and masthead tri-colour light. If the old ones are not burned out they can be kept as spares.

At the same time, all pulleys and blocks on the mast, especially those above deck level, should be checked, serviced or replaced as necessary. Unless running rigging is reasonably new then it will not last the entire trip.

NEW SAILS OR OLD?

New sails are not always necessary. On *Mintaka* I replaced both the genoa and the mainsail. The new sails were triple stitched and could stop an artillery shell. They gave no trouble. *Margo* used the sails that came with her; they were, I guess, ten years old, single stitched and of uncertain pedigree. They too were trouble free. Early reefing reduces wear and tear. Sails die from chafe and sunlight. Avoid chafe by keeping the main clear of the spreaders, topping lifts, jackstays, and sheets lying across a sail. Stitch or tape every tear, however insignificant, the instant you spot it. The only protection against UV is to cover sails the moment you arrive in an anchorage.

If you have roller headsails a huge sail wardrobe is unnecessary though a spare genoa is useful, especially in the trades, and if you wish, a cruising chute, gennaker or spinnaker. I have never carried a storm jib or a trysail and never missed them.

A second spinnaker pole is useful in the Trades. If the price of buying a new pole shocks, then beg, borrow or scrounge a couple of end fittings and visit your local aluminium distributor. Somewhere in the depths of his shed he will have a length of thick-walled, aluminium tubing that is exactly what you need and a few minutes with a drill and a pop-riveter will produce a serviceable spinnaker pole.

SELF-STEERING GEAR

Unless there is a need to keep the crew gainfully employed some form of self-steering is essential. The tyranny of steering a compass course watch-and-watch takes the fun out of sailing. It has been done, can be done but it is done better by a self-steering unit. Of all the additions and alterations made during the refit, installing a reliable self-steering system is one of the most important.

POWERED AUTOHELMS

The initial choice is between a powered autohelm or a windvane. In an autohelm system, any deviation from the desired compass course is detected and an electric motor pulls or pushes a rod or pumps hydraulic fluid until the boat returns to the chosen course. Most units can be fitted with a small windvane transducer that allows a course to be steered relative to the wind. Some systems can be integrated with the ship's instruments, including the GPS, so that the autohelm will make the necessary course corrections without being told.

Choose the right autohelm for your yacht and the sailing you plan to do. A unit that is fine for occasional weekend or coastal cruising may not be able to withstand the demands of an ocean passage. Reliability is very important. If your system cannot be trusted to steer a course in all wind and sea conditions, then life will be disagreeable. If it breaks down, then its electronic innards are beyond the capabilities of most yachtsmen to repair. When it is working it devours a great chunk of your energy budget, typically between three and five amps an hour, varying with factors such as sea conditions, sail trim and the amount of weather helm.

WINDVANE SELF-STEERING

Windvanes always steer a course relative to the wind. While this makes for lazy sail trimming it does mean that if the wind direction changes then you follow the wind, and it is not unknown to come on deck and find the boat steering the reciprocal of the desired course. This is a small penalty to pay for a system that imposes no drain on your battery.

Windvane systems first appeared in the early 1900s and attracted most interest from model yachtsmen. Half a century later Francis Chichester returned the compliment when he developed his Miranda self-steering gear for the first OSTAR by watching model yachts race across a pond. That race introduced windvanes to the sailing public and soon any yacht with pretensions to long-distance sailing had one hanging from its stern. This is one of the differences between windvanes and autohelms. Windvanes are big, obvious. Fitting one can be a challenge to your ingenuity and depends not only on the shape of your vessel's stern but on what is already hanging there in the form of mizzen booms, boarding ladders, swim platforms, rudders and davits.

All windvanes have a vane to sense the wind direction. This may be horizontally or vertically mounted. A vertical vane weather-cocks like the vane on a church steeple, a horizontal vane falls over to one side or the other and is reckoned to be more sensitive and powerful. Once a change in relative wind is detected, that information is used to deliver the power to steer a yacht.

Windvanes work best with a balanced sail plan and their efficiency falls off as weather

(or lee) helm grows. This means reefing early and upright sailing, which increases the comfort factor but will not win races. On a run wind passing over the vane is reduced by the boat speed and, again, efficiency falls off.

The simplest systems use the vane to pull lines attached to the tiller. Many years ago I installed this type of system, convinced by its claims to be very powerful, highly sensitive and having steered at least one yacht across the Atlantic. I learned the hard way that it worked only in a gale or when approached in a threatening manner with a hammer.

A trim tab linked to the vane can be attached to a transom-hung rudder. This avoids separate steering lines to the tiller and reduces cockpit clutter. It is also a useful system if you have

I used the French servo-pendulum Navik self-steering system on Mintaka. *With this type, the vane turns a paddle and the water rushing across causes the paddle to swing one side or the other until the boat is back on course.*

a centre cockpit that would otherwise require extremely long steering lines. An alternative for centre cockpit yachts without a transom-hung rudder is to fit a system which includes an auxiliary rudder. This steers the yacht while the main rudder is used to reduce weather helm. These systems work well but reversing with the auxiliary rudder in place can be exciting.

A popular form of windvane is the servo-pendulum system where the vane turns a paddle and the water rushing across causes the paddle to swing to one side or another until the vessel is back on course.

Windvanes are simple, and once tuned to you and your yacht, reliable. Generally they can be repaired on board but they work only if there is a wind. If you wish to motor through calms then an autohelm is necessary. With a little ingenuity one of the push-rod type autohelms can be rigged so that it is linked to the windvane and pushes it from side to side instead of the tiller. This reduces both the loads on, and power consumption of, the autohelm.

The choice between autohelm or windvane is not straightforward. Every system or combination of systems has its adherents who swear on a stack of almanacs that their particular arrangement is the only sensible option. In practice it appears that the more powerful a system (autohelm or windvane) is then the better it works.

The price of a good windvane system will buy two or three autohelms and some argue that it is cheaper and wiser to buy two autohelms and have 100% redundancy, for two-thirds of the cost, than to rely upon one windvane system. It is an idea worth considering but if you opt for this, then you place a premium on the capacity of the ship's batteries and reliability of your battery-charging systems.

ENGINES

Engines are mainly used for entering and leaving harbour and keeping batteries charged. Motoring through calms or motor sailing in light winds is now common and many yachts carry fuel for a range of over 1000 miles under power.

OUTBOARD ENGINES

These do have disadvantages: they are greedy for petrol, and fuel storage is a problem both from the space demanded and the danger of spillages and fumes. Petrol may be less readily available in marinas. Also, outboards rarely produce enough power for recharging batteries. The greatest advantage of out-boards is that if the prop is fouled, it is simple to raise the engine and clear the obstruction.

DIESEL ENGINES

Most yachts have diesel engines either as saildrives or for driving a prop shaft. Modern diesels are very reliable. If faults occur it is likely to be in the fuel system, starter motor or alternator. Good pre-voyage servicing and a full spares kit is essential including oil, filter, fan belts and hoses. Fitting a warp cutter to the prop shaft could prove useful.

Consider fitting an extra fuel tank in a locker to avoid having too many spare cans. Use a siphon pump for fuel transfer.

AWNINGS

In the tropics lounging in the cockpit adds a touch of gracious living but only if there is an awning to shade you from the sun. This can be anything from a simple boom tent to a sophisticated combination of fold-away bimini with an awning fitted with opening windows and electric lights.

On *Mintaka* the cost of a sailmaker-made boom tent was so outrageous that I bought a heavy duty (so called) mail-order tarpaulin at a twentieth of the price and threw it over the boom as a simple A-tent covering the cockpit. It worked and lasted 15 months. For *Margo* I had an awning made that hung underneath the boom fastened to the A-frame on the stern and roll bar at the front of the cockpit. A tendency to flap in the wind was reduced by lashing lengths of plastic water piping across the ends as spreaders.

A plastic skin fitting in its centre took a hose that led to the water tank. When it rained I would slacken off the awning, create a hollow and allow water to run to the tank. It worked brilliantly but living in the cockpit with a hose dangling down the middle is a nuisance. I should have placed the skin fitting at one end.

If you have the space, then have an awning that can remain in place when underway. It will need to be taken down in strong winds but at all other times it will be much appreciated by all on board.

A pramhood (our American cousins call it

I very successfully used an inexpensive, heavy duty, mail-order tarpaulin as a simple A-tent over the boom, providing shelter for the cockpit.

a 'dodger') is essential. It provides shelter in heavy weather and protects the cabin from spray when you open the hatch to take a look around. There was not room to fit one on *Mintaka* and its absence probably explains why I spent so little time on deck in heavy weather.

Plastic windows in pramhoods become smoky in the sun. I like the idea of replacing the canvas pramhood with a version in GRP. This will allow me to fit at least one toughened glass window and improve forward visibility. It will also allow me to make better use of the space underneath the pramhood.

GOALPOSTS

The competition for deck space to fit radars, antennas, wind generators, solar panels is intense. On *Margo* my solution was to fit an A-frame or 'goalposts' (see photo below) on the stern. This is a U-shaped arrangement of stainless steel (it could also be made in aluminium) that carries equipment that would otherwise clutter the deck or mast. I found room for a spare tri-colour light (if the masthead light failed then I would not have to climb the mast at sea to repair it) and a strobe light. I know that using a strobe light as a steaming light is wrong but there are times when I rate being seen at night above legality.

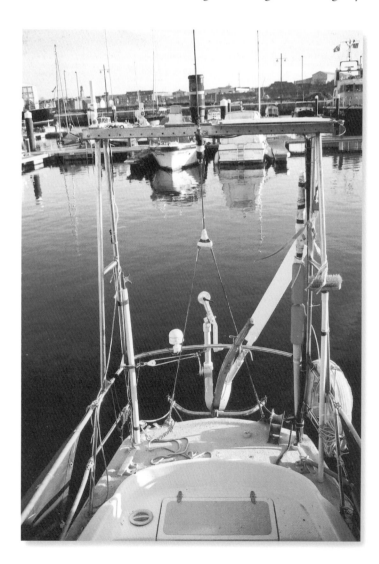

The problem of what to do with all the assorted antennas and lights can be easily solved by fitting a U-shaped set of 'goalposts' on the stern.

3 Cruising Essentials

As the boat will become your home whilst afloat, you need to think carefully about your individual needs below decks – both basic and recreational (the trip is meant to be fun). Can these needs be accommodated? Ask yourself a few questions:

- Are there enough comfy bunks?
- Is the living area adequate for eating, relaxing, personal hobbies and chartwork?
- Is the galley up to the cook's specifications?
- Are the water tanks sufficient for an Atlantic crossing?
- Is there enough locker space for clothes, food, books and personal possessions?
- Are the ablution facilities up to scratch for a long passage?
- Is the lighting and ventilation adequate?
- Will the below-deck areas be safe during a blow?

A COMFY BUNK

Top of my priority list is a comfortable bunk where I can stretch out and sleep warm, safe and secure regardless of the weather. You must be able to stay in your bunk without hanging on for dear life. Quarter berths are good but not the whole answer, for the top half of your body can slip out. Lee cloths or lee-boards along the length of the bunk deep enough to prevent you from being thrown out are best. I like lee cloths. They are more comfortable than lee-boards, and if attached top and bottom towards the hull, they form a cuddly, secure, cocoon. Lee cloths must be strongly made. The usual eyelet in the corner of a hem is fine for a static load but if you are thrown against them the eyelets will pop out and the cloth will tear. The corners of lee

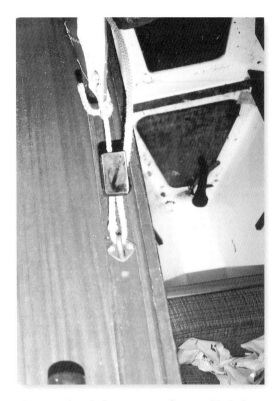

If you use lee cloths, you must fit some kind of quick release, such as this clam cleat, to allow you to escape from your bunk quickly if necessary.

cloths should have a strong resemblance to a storm jib clew. The lines holding the lee cloth in position must be fitted with some form of quick release to allow you to escape from your bunk and dash to the cockpit. For the same reason a duvet is preferable to a sleeping bag.

LIVING ON BOARD

On *Mintaka* I found the living conditions to be similar to those found in a small tent; OK for a single-hander, perhaps, but families need

An essential part of the cruising dream: sitting comfortably on deck enjoying a meal with friends.

reasonable space and it needs to be well-planned and adaptable if the crossing is going to be enjoyable for everyone. Homes have separate rooms for different functions and so should your cruiser. A family trying to eat, sleep, work and play in one area is asking for conflict. So try, as far as possible, to keep sleeping and living areas separate and ensure that people have their own 'space' or bolthole if needed. You may find that you opt for different arrangements at different times; for example a couple may use the forepeak as bedroom in harbour, leaving the saloon for socialising while sleeping in the more comfortable saloon or settee berths at sea. A family, on the other hand will need separate cabins for parents and children whether at sea or in harbour. Think ahead to what everyone's needs will be during weeks afloat.

Safety below
Careful consideration should be given to move- ment below decks. Do people have to climb round the cook or navigator when they are at work? Does a table in the saloon cause gridlock? Are there enough grab handles below deck so you can move around safely? If you are thrown across the cabin by a rogue wave, what will hit you? Will lockers fly open and sauce- pans become missiles? Hard, sharp corners and edges break ribs, backs and fracture skulls. Is the cabin sole non-slip, especially when wet or greasy?

Are you sitting comfortably? Francis Chichester sailed with a gimballed chair to guarantee a comfy seat, but on most yachts the choice is between sitting to windward, feet braced or in the depths of a leeward settee. Finding every-one a snug, secure seat with sufficient space to eat or read is no problem in harbour but what about at sea? Life below decks must be simple, safe and secure.

Lighting and ventilation
Although they give a kinder light, paraffin lamps are mostly restricted to the cockpit at night when at anchor. Fluorescent strip lights give good general illumination below decks and small tungsten lights provide individual lighting for bunks, galley or chart table.

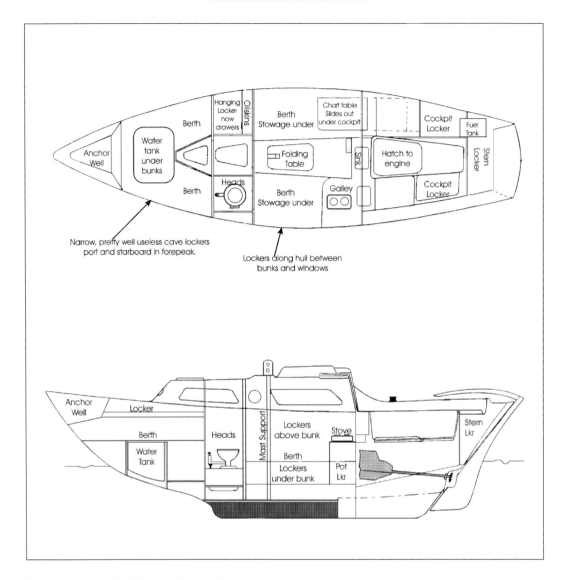

Below-deck plans for Margo, *a Dockerel 27.*

However, fluorescent lights do interfere with MF and HF radio reception so they will need to be switched off when listening to the weather forecast.

It is easy to provide enough fresh air below decks at sea, but in harbour it is a different tale. Within minutes of anchoring in the tropics, the cabin will become an airless hotbox. The step is to spread an awning which will cover as much of the deck and cockpit as possible. This not only keeps the sun off the deck but drives cool air between the awning and the deck. Next, open the

hatches and, if necessary, fit wind- sails to push air through the boat. This should make life bearable.

THE GALLEY

After sleep, my next priority is food. It is important that, regardless of sea conditions, you are able to prepare decent hot food and drink. Ideally, the stove should be gimballed. Some vessels have fixed stoves and rely on fiddle rails or pan holders to keep pots in place but on most yachts at sea, the motion is so lively that unless single burner stoves and very deep pots are used, this system would see the food on the cabin sole. Even a well-gimballed stove needs good fiddle rails or pan holders.

When working in the galley you must be able to devote both hands to cooking and not need to hang on for dear life. On *Margo* I thought I could wedge myself between the steps leading into the cabin and the front of the galley. I could, but not when there was a sea running. Ever tried peeling a potato one-handed? Mealtimes could be messy and frustrating and I had only myself to blame.

It is easiest and safest to work in the galley sitting down. A strap across the galley, against which the cook can lean, is good; you could also install the stove and work surfaces at a level which allows the cook to sit down on a settee.

On both *Mintaka* and *Margo*, a stove, sink and small workspace passed for a galley but on bigger boats, galleys are as well-equipped as any shoreside kitchen. Fridges and freezers are commonplace and microwave cookers, some running at 12 volts DC and others on rectifiers, are appearing on more and more yachts; some yachts even have a washing machine.

Check how efficient your fridge and freezer are at keeping the cold in and the heat out, for in the tropics the difference between the temperature inside a fridge and the outside air is much greater than in European waters. Everything works harder and the drain on your battery increases. It might be possible to uprate the insulation or to change to top-opening rather than side-opening fridge and freezer to prevent cold air escaping each time the fridge is used.

I am in two minds about the value of a sink on small boats. They are very useful in harbour or at anchor where throwing a bucket full of dirty water over the side is regarded as anti-social behaviour. If you have a sink then it should be as deep as possible to hold a fair amount of water when heeled, and if possible, it should be located on the centreline for the same reason. It is a fair bet

that the sink outlet will be below the waterline and it will be necessary to fit a pump to prevent the sink flooding the boat. Pumps do not like kitchen waste and many an unhappy and messy hour can be spent unblocking the pump. It is a task that runs the unpleasantness of clearing the heads a close second. Buckets are much simpler and are one hole less in the hull.

COOKING FUELS

On *Mintaka* I had a paraffin stove. Despite a tendency to flare up during the ignition stage it was marvellous, even though friends claimed that North Sea oil rigs used it to check their position. Finding fuel was never a problem and I avoided all the problems associated with using gas. Paraffin may smell if you spill it but it will not blow up the boat.

Alcohol stoves are an alternative. They are safe, but in Europe finding fuel in sufficient quantities is difficult, also alcohol or paraffin stoves with an oven are rare. If you wish to bake or roast then it is necessary to use a metal box that sits onto the top of the stove. This glows in the night and brands anyone who falls against it.

Like most European yachts *Margo* was fitted with a butane gas supply, but in the USA butane is almost unknown and probably unobtainable south of the Canaries. An exception is the French Antilles where Camping Gaz is obtainable. Once away from the European mainland, bottle exchange is rare and when your gas bottles are refilled in the Caribbean you will usually receive propane, butane occasionally, or an LPG cocktail sometimes called 'cooking gas'.

Cylinders are tested at regular intervals and the next test date appears on the aluminium tare disk that comes with every cylinder. Before leaving Europe be sure that your cylinders are in good condition and that they will not need testing before your return. Suppliers may refuse to refill scruffy or out-of date-cylinders.

There is normally little choice in the matter but cylinders should never be completely filled. In Europe a 'full' cylinder is

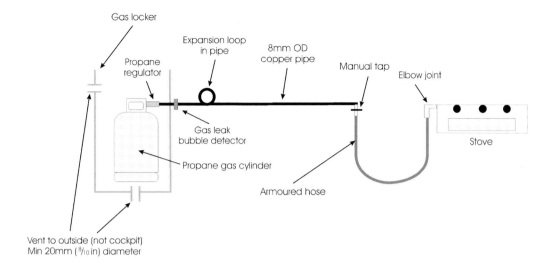

Gas locker

Expansion loop
in pipe

8mm OD
copper pipe

Propane
regulator

Manual tap

Elbow joint

Gas leak
bubble detector

Stove

Propane gas cylinder

Armoured hose

Vent to outside (not cockpit)
Min 20mm ($^8/_{10}$ in) diameter

Fig 4 *Liquid Propane Gas (LPG) installation. 1 Fit compression joints where the pipe leaves the gas locker to give gas-tight exit. 2 Use plastic sleeves to protect pipe where it passes through bulkheads. 3 Support the pipe with pipe clips every 8in (200mm). 4 Do not run pipe through bilges or where it may be damaged.*

LPG GAS CONSUMPTION

Set to 'high' a single gas burner will use about 170 grams (6 oz) of gas per hour. At this rate a kilogram of gas will last a shade under six hours. The exact figure is 5 hours 54 minutes but such accuracy is unwise for burners are rarely set to high all the time and different burners use fuel at different rates. An oven or grill probably uses twice as much as a single burner. Check what weight of gas one of your bottles holds when full and calculate how long it should last.

It is unlikely that you will start a passage with all gas bottles completely full. It is good practice to have three bottles on board, one in use and two in reserve. There is the temptation to install the biggest bottles possible but remember you will have to take them ashore and carry them around when they are being refilled.

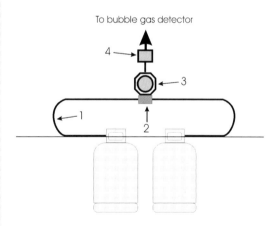

To bubble gas detector

Fig 5 *Two-bottle LPG installation. 1 High pressure hose with appropriate end fittings. 2 Double-wall-block propane manifold with non-return valve and bracket. 3 Propane regulator. 4 Shut-off valve.*

80% full but in the tropics it is safer to reduce this figure to 70%.

Propane is stored at a much higher pressure than butane and I gather that while a propane regulator may not like butane gas it will handle it safely, but a butane regulator will throw a wobbly if fed propane. Butane has a higher calorific value than propane and burns with a hotter flame. If your stove is not rated for butane (modern stoves can usually handle either fuel) then this may warp the unit, buckle oven doors or burn out the burners. I changed to propane but carried a butane regulator just in case.

Many production yachts come with built-in gas lockers that meet the regulations on gas safety and are sized round a standard Camping Gaz bottle. Once in the Caribbean, Camping Gaz is readily available only in French possessions like Martinique. Elsewhere finding refills is a problem. The simplest solution is to buy a propane bottle and regulator, but standard propane bottles will not fit into the smaller Camping Gaz locker. In some American yachting magazines custom-made propane bottles are advertised but they are expensive. Other options are to modify the existing locker, build a new locker, or carry a propane cylinder on deck and run a new gas line to the stove.

Refilling Camping Gaz bottles is not easy as the fittings in most filling stations are for propane bottles. One solution I saw was to remove the insides from a Camping Gaz regulator so that gas could flow into the bottle and on the outlet (now the inlet) side attach a short length of hose with a propane adaptor on the end. This allows the Camping Gaz bottle to be filled with propane but I suspect that it is a technique which would have any gas engineer expressing his disapproval from behind a distant, sandbagged, blast proof shelter.

I do not know the answer to this dilemma but it is a point that yachts fitted for Camping Gaz should explore before sailing, so that modifications to their gas supply can be made in good time.

Propane and butane have different fittings to attach the regulator to the bottle. Propane

ENTERTAINMENT AT SEA

In heavy weather it is amazing how going below, crawling into your bunk and playing a favourite tape can make the weather seem a distant memory. If you do not already have a stereo system then it is worth fitting one. The type used in cars with tape and CD decks is best. Second-hand models can sometimes be picked up from the small ads in the local paper or from firms who specialise in installing sound systems in cars. Be warned that the cost of the music centre rarely includes the speakers; buy those speakers that will survive in salty air. It is important to install it where it is least likely to become wet. This is not as easy as it sounds as such spots are scarce and there is other equipment, like VHF, HF radios and radars, claiming priority.

Encourage crew members to bring their portable stereos with them so they can listen to their choice of music without disturbing everyone else.

cylinder valves have a female 'POL' connection with a $\frac{5}{8}$ in BSP female left-hand thread. Butane cylinders have a $\frac{5}{8}$ in BSP male left-hand thread. But there are also differences between different suppliers in different countries. It is important to always use the right connector between the regulator and the gas bottle and if you expect to change to a different type of bottle en route then it may be best to use some variation on the two-bottle LPG installation (Fig 5) and all you will need to change is the connector to the bottle.

American yachtsmen heading towards Europe should give this serious consideration for the near complete absence of bottle refill schemes and the prevalence of Camping Gaz in Mediterranean areas means that their easiest solution may be to buy a bottle of gas, enter the bottle exchange scheme while in European waters, and then trade in the European bottle before leaving for home.

It is not really necessary to have a dedicated chart table if you have a good area of bulkhead, most of your navigation equipment can be fitted on the wall.

A total of an hour a day spent navigating – a fraction of the time spent working in the galley or lying in your bunk – and yet many chart tables occupy a quarter of the main cabin, holy ground that may not be put to any other use.

With GPS on board it is hard to spend an hour a day navigating. Everything is done by the box on the wall which, if asked nicely, will tell you where you are, where you are going, what course to steer and when you will arrive. Who needs a chart table or a navigator?

Of course it is nice to spread charts out on a table and see where you are going and when making a coastal passage there must be a chart with your position marked up laid out on the table, but any table with a fiddle rail will do the job. It does not have to be a dedicated chart table.

RADAR AND RADAR DETECTORS

Coming home in 1996, the last few days towards Falmouth were spent in thick fog. The Western Approaches were crowded and fishing fleets weaved about like drunks in rush hour traffic. I knew that I was surrounded but I had no idea where other ships were or what course they were steering. I would have sold my grandmother for a radar set. All I could do was sit in the cockpit ready to run for my life.

I had ruled radar out partly on cost and partly on the grounds that I could not carry enough batteries to power it up long enough to be useful. Since 1995, radar sets have been reduced both in price and power demands. In sleep or standby mode they make two or three sweeps at predetermined intervals and only power up if they see a target and even then battery drain is low. The remaining argument against them is that, once in the Caribbean, fog is unknown but heavy tropical rain can give a very good imitation of fog, and when night sailing, it is common to meet unlit local

THE NAVIGATION AREA

The navigation area is a major selling point of many cruising yachts, with a full-sized chart table surrounded by instruments and radios giving a fair impersonation of the *Starship Enterprise*. On ocean passages, navigation is a part-time activity and never justifies the exclusive use of space that could be put to better use.

In the days when positions were fixed using a sextant, the sum of the daily navigational duties consisted of taking one sight in the morning, another in the afternoon (or noon), sitting down to work out both sights and running the morning sight forward until it crossed with the afternoon sight to give a position. This took about half an hour. Occasionally, for fun, star sights would be taken at dusk and another half-hour or so spent doing simple arithmetic and plotting.

boats. If you must make a landfall in the islands at night, then a radar set is a pearl without price provided the screen is where it can be seen by those on watch. This means the cockpit. Running up and down between the cockpit and cabin can waste precious time.

Instead of a radar set I carried a radar detector (see Appendix D), which could be left on all the time. This gives a warning bleep every time its antenna is hit by another vessel's radar beam and gives a good idea of its relative bearing. With some practice it was even possible to make a fair guess as to the target's course and whether or not it was approaching or moving away. In mid-ocean, where traffic was scarce, it is splendid and gives early warning of any approaching vessel.

Radar detectors have their drawbacks. Firstly, they rely on other vessels switching on their radar set. Not all do this. Secondly, there is no indication of range. If a radar detector does show the relative strength of the radar signal, there is no way of telling if it is a distant high-powered radar or a nearby low-powered radar. High power military radars light up radar detectors from miles over the horizon and look as if they are about to run you down. Thirdly, when there is a lot of traffic then if the radar detector is not confused by multiple signals, I am.

A radar detector and radar set is a great power-saving combination. In normal conditions you can rely on the radar detector to tell you if there is a vessel nearby and only power up the radar set if in doubt.

POWER TO THE PEOPLE

Radios, radars, plotters, computers, auto-pilots, fridges, freezers, washing machines and micro-waves running all day, every day, take your energy budget far above demands of the normal summer cruise and you cannot count upon shore-based power supplies to keep the ship's batteries topped up. Instead, you must rely either on the engine's alternator or some combination of onboard battery-charging systems. Batteries are the backbone of your electrical system. Lose them and everything stops. Refitting is a good time to make sure that you have the right batteries aboard, together with the means of keeping them charged.

TYPES OF BATTERY

There are four basic types of battery:

- Car batteries
- Marine batteries
- Engine start batteries
- Deep discharge batteries

Good marine batteries are more expensive and are supposedly more robust than car batteries. Both types are constructed in the same way and sometimes the greatest difference between them is more in price and labelling than quality.

Engine start batteries deliver a blast of power, quickly replaced from the engine alternator, and are used to start engines. Deep discharge (or deep cycle) batteries give steady power for modest (compared to the demands of starting an engine) loads for long periods between charges. They are for domestic use and should not be used for starting engines.

BATTERY CAPACITY

Battery size or capacity is measured in ampere (amp) hours. A 100-amp hour battery can pump out one amp for a hundred hours or 100 amps for one hour or any ratio of amps and hours as long as the answer does not exceed 100. The usual 25-watt masthead tri-colour bulb draws just over 2 amps so a 100-amp hour battery will keep it shining for just under 50 hours. The higher the amp hour figure the more power the battery contains, the bigger it will be and the more it will cost.

On *Mintaka*, power supplies were simple. Having no need for an engine start battery I installed one deep cycle battery. *Margo*, with her diesel engine, was more complicated. I bought separate engine and domestic batteries and installed a switching system that

Boats rafted up together in the busy harbour at Funchal.

allowed me to use the deep discharge battery solely for domestic use and yet still charge it from the engine alternator when it was running.

The charge remaining in a battery can be checked in two ways. Firstly, the probes of a multi-meter set to the correct voltage range can be placed across the battery contacts and the battery voltage read. The higher the voltage, the more charge there is in the battery. Secondly, it can be checked by a hydrometer. Each 12 volt battery has six cells each nominally of 2.1 volts when fully charged. A hydrometer measures the specific gravity of the electrolyte in each cell. It is a glass tube with a narrow opening at one end and a bulb at the other. Inside the tube is a small, weighted float graduated to read specific gravity; the higher the reading then the more the charge.

Check the specific gravity cell by cell. Every cell should be about the same specific gravity but if one is 50 or more points lower than the rest then it is possibly 'bad'. Sometimes plates buckle and touch or a build-up of sulphate can short out a cell. Either effectively kills the battery. Usually there is little that can be done but it is nice to know where the fault lies.

If you have opted for sealed or gel batteries then using a hydrometer is out of the question as is carrying out a cell-by-cell check using a multi-meter unless the battery has external straps connecting each cell to its neighbour on top of the battery case. This lets you use a multi-meter to check the voltage cell by cell. Most batteries have internal straps.

Batteries need tender loving care if they are to work for their advertised working life. They should be fastened down in an easily accessible, well-ventilated battery box, their terminals kept clean, free of corrosion (petroleum jelly is good) and their charge checked daily. No battery, even deep cycle batteries, likes being run flat. They should be given a charge at least every couple of days. The usual advice includes keeping batteries horizontal (wry smile from most yachtsmen) to prevent electro-lyte spilling out or flooding from one cell to another. Even sealed batteries can leak for they have vents to allow the charging gases to escape. All this is a counsel of perfection. Batteries are abused and continue working but mistreatment shortens their useful life.

THE ENERGY BUDGET

I was shocked when I worked out how much electrical power *Margo* consumed in a typical day at sea (see Appendix E). There were the ship's instruments, the VHF radio on stand-by and talk time, listening on the SSB, the stereo, domestic and navigation lights, and the laptop computer. And I did not have a SSB transceiver, fridge, freezer, watermaker, electric pumps, spreader lights, windlasses or electric bilge and water pumps common on many yachts, and on long passages I did not use the autohelm.

To work out a yacht's energy budget, make a list of all electrical equipment and note how much power (watts) each item takes to run. Next calculate how many amps it takes to work by using the formula:

Amps = Watts divided by Volts

Since most boats run on a 12 volt circuit this becomes

Amps = Watts divided by 12

The answer to this sum is multiplied by the number of hours each item is used in a typical day. This gives the daily amp hours for each item. Add the amp hours together, allowing 20% for inaccuracies and over-optimism. On *Margo* it was necessary to put in nearly 80 amp hours a day to keep the battery fully charged. I found it useful to prepare separate energy budgets for when I was on passage and when I was at anchor.

Do not confuse your energy budget with battery capacity. It is not a one-to-one relationship. Much depends on how often and how much you charge your batteries. Your charging regime should aim to keep your batteries at a minimum of 30–50% charge, higher if you can manage it.

The energy budget for your boat will almost certainly be higher than you first thought, probably between 100–150 amp hours a day and this turns thoughts to ways of keeping the batteries charged. Failure to meet your energy budget means turning equipment off to meet your reduced circumstances or accepting a return to a simpler age when your batteries run flat.

Battery-charging on a motor vessel presents no difficulties. On a yacht where there may be only one battery charging session a day to supplement intermittent systems like wind generators or solar panels it is prudent to add another 30% to your energy budget and use this figure to decide your battery capacity. In my case the sums told me that I needed a 110 amp hour battery.

CHARGING BATTERIES

Wind generators

On *Mintaka*, battery-charging had always been a problem. The outboard could power the autohelm and that was about all. I tried a wind generator but this proved a disappointment. It was fine for recharging the battery between weekend cruises but it could not meet even my limited demands on a three-week cruise. Its rated output was 2.5 amps but it rarely exceeded one amp and then only in strong winds. A feature of all wind generators is that in light winds and calms they do not work.

Mounting it safely had not been easy. It sat on top of an 8-foot pole on the stern. Anything lower and there was a risk of my head making contact with the blades, and the pole had to be stayed just like a miniature mizzen to prevent it swaying.

By the time I came to refit *Margo* I had lost faith in wind generators and struck them off my list of possibilities. This was wrong. They have improved by leaps and bounds and there is a wide selection on the market that will meet most needs.

Water-towed generators

A close cousin to the wind generator is the water-towed generator. These are powerful beasts capable of meeting all but the most outrageous demands. Power is not free and in this case it costs about half a knot of boat speed. Since I reckoned to average about three knots, cutting it by 15% was too high a price to pay. Besides, it would only produce power underway and not in harbour or at anchor. Some towed generators solve this problem by providing a kit that allows you to temporarily convert the water-towed generator to a wind generator and hang it in the rigging.

Solar panels

Solar panels are a good answer. They do not require a complicated mounting system or affect sailing performance but they do demand acres of flat space and on a 20-foot yacht free space, never mind flat space, is in short supply. I bought a 35-watt panel that sat on top of the newly sealed down forehatch and it worked well.

No solar panel works in the dark. They work best when pointed directly at the sun and I have seen yachts where solar panels have been mounted on swinging arms or poles with universal joints to make sure the panel can always point at the sun.

Engine alternators

Since *Margo* has an inboard diesel engine uprating the alternator was a possibility but I settled for adding a solar panel, reasoning that two independent generating systems were better than one super-powerful system, and as a bonus, I would need to run the engine only every other day. This proved a wise decision. There were two occasions when, for extended periods at sea, the engine would not start and I relied solely upon the solar panel and wished that I had invested in a small petrol generator.

BATTERY MANAGEMENT SYSTEMS

You may wish to consider fitting a battery management system. There is a good selection, each slightly different from the other, but all aim to make your alternator recharge your batteries as quickly as possible and then to keep them charged.

INVERTERS

At the same time as sorting out batteries and battery charging, think about an inverter. This will convert the battery's 12 volt direct current to domestic alternating current. In the UK this is 240 volts at 50Hz. This allows you to use domestic appliances and the type of domestic appliance you wish to use will determine the type of inverter you need. An inverter that will comfortably handle a laptop computer and printer will baulk at an electric drill. It is wise to buy an oversized inverter capable of handling several hundred watts.

No system of power generating is ideal, they all have drawbacks, but there are two guiding principles to follow. First, over-rather than under-estimate your power consumption. Second, two independent systems are good, three is even better. Not only will the advantages of one system cancel the draw-backs of the other(s) but it would be bad luck to lose every system.

LIVING WITH A POWER BLACK OUT

Murphy's law still says this is possible. If all electrical power were lost, could you continue sailing? Not long ago this would have been a ridiculous question as yachts happily crossed the ocean without electrics or electronics. Not now. What about something as simple as navigation lights? The small dry cell emergency navigation lights are a nod towards obeying the Collision Regulations and are invisible a few feet away. A paraffin lantern is great for giving a soft light in the cabin but no better at providing light for being seen. A paraffin pressure lantern like a Tilley lamp is great but it uses much more fuel. But how many yachts carry a paraffin lantern or Tilley lamp? Battery-operated strobes running for hours on one battery are a better answer if you carry enough batteries or keep a night time watch and switch it on whenever another vessel is seen.

The battery life of a handheld GPS unit is now over 20 hours and most yachts carry at least one handheld set as a back-up to the main GPS unit. On passage it is not necessary to run it continuously; once a day, at noon, is enough to see where you are and make any course corrections. One set of batteries should be enough for the entire trip. Most of the islands have aero radio beacons so that an old battery-operated RDF set might come in handy.

There will be no log, no wind instrument-ation, echo-sounder or radios but if you have made a point of charging the handheld VHF then you will be able to speak to other stations. Even if it is not switched on the battery will slowly lose its charge. A small SSB receiver will run for between seven and ten hours on one set of dry cell batteries. This limits your listening to weather forecasts.

With a 35-watt solar panel, a complete power failure on *Margo* was unlikely. Allowing for over-estimating its efficiency I reckoned it would put about 15 amp hours a day into the battery and I used this as the basis for my power miser budget which told me what I could run and how long I could run it. This planning paid off. I lost the engine, and its alternator, twice.

Losing power ought to be an inconvenience rather than a problem but if you carry most of your food in the fridge or freezer or

---

THE ENGINE AND ITS FUEL SUPPLY

The engine should be serviced with special attention being given to hoses and drive belts. These should be checked, replaced if necessary, and spares ordered. Give some thought to fuel supplies. It is common to see blue-water yachts with cans of fuel lining the side decks. One difficulty in carrying fuel this way is transferring the fuel from the can to the tank in a seaway. If there is space it makes sense to fit a second tank with its own fuel lines and filters. This reduces the problems of fuel transfer and if there is a problem with one fuel line the engine can be kept running using the second tank while the first is repaired.

if you are relying on a water maker or an electrically-pumped water system, without any form of manual back-up, then you do have problems that can only be solved by having multiple, independent power generating systems each capable of providing enough power to meet your minimum requirements.

SKIN FITTINGS

Skin fittings have a very low failure rate and are taken for granted. Before sailing they should all be taken off, checked and refitted. Any that are more than a few years old or of uncertain age should be replaced.

Every skin fitting, even those above the waterline, should have a valve, which allows it to be shut, instantly and without fuss. I like ball valves. Sometimes the wheel on a gate valve spins lock-to-lock and does nothing. You may think it is working perfectly but the valve is either permanently open or shut. The pretty red wheel handles are only painted mild steel and rust until they crumble in your hand. If you like gate valves then carry a selection of spare handles. A suitably-sized wooden plug should be taped to the line leading to every valve so that should the valve fail then you can quickly reduce the inflow of water to manageable proportions.

THE STERN GLAND

The stern gland on the prop shaft internal engines should be checked and if of the traditional type the packing replaced.

RUDDER TUBES

If the rudder shaft passes through the hull in an internal tube, inspect where it passes through the hull. Once returning home across the North Sea from Holland we discovered rather more of the North Sea inside *Mintaka* than was good for our peace of mind. The rudder tube could only be approached by squeezing through a small hatch and crawling underneath the cockpit.

This was impossible for my well-endowed 16 stones but fortunately my crew came from a line of Northumberland miners and needed only minimal encouragement to burrow his way through. He reported the rudder tube was splitting where it went through the hull and made a temporary repair using tape intended for rainwater guttering. If you have to do any work to the rudder tube then the aim should be to spread the load over as wide an area of the hull as possible.

While you are doing this, check the rudder bearings and replace them if necessary and order some spares. They will be needed.

FRESH WATER TANKS

Mintaka had one six-gallon fresh water tank under the forepeak V-berth. At half a gallon a day, this gave me twelve days' water, which was not enough. The answer was two five-gallon plastic water cans carried in the cockpit and half a dozen collapsible cans (bought in a sale at the local camping store) in the forepeak. Together they gave more than enough for a transatlantic crossing.

By chance I had stumbled onto a system of water storage that obeyed two very important rules. By carrying water in several tanks, losing one or two tanks might be inconvenient but not disastrous. Secondly, I was able to monitor my water consumption and make sure I was not exceeding my daily ration.

Other options included a water maker that would meet my daily ration and keep the tank topped up, or installing another tank. I could not afford the first and did not have room for the second, though a two-tank system is a rough and ready way of measuring consumption. It is tempting to fit a collapsible water tank as a second tank. They are convenient and easy to install but though they are made of very tough material no matter how well they are fastened down they do chafe and, eventually, leak. A rigid tank with all the problems of fitting it into the space available is better.

Once away from the Channel coast, marinas and harbours have water points but not hoses. A long hose with a selection (this grows as you go) of different tap (faucet) fittings is essential if you wish to fill your tanks without fuss. I use a roll flat hose because it takes up less room but it is a nuisance to use. It must always be fully unrolled before use and, when finished, rolling up must be done carefully if it is to fit on its holder.

At anchor in the Caribbean, tanks are either filled from a water barge that comes alongside or by ferrying plastic jerry cans to and from the shore. Water is not free and not always potable so always ask before you fill your cans. Even if it is potable it is a good idea to add about a teaspoon of chlorine (chlorine bleach will do) or iodine to every 40 gallons (180 litres) every time you fill up. A good in-line water filter should be fitted between the water tank and the taps.

Tropical squalls can replenish water tanks. I have managed this at anchor but never underway, though I have filled a bucket simply by putting it into the cockpit. Canting up the boom and catching the run-off in a bucket is another possibility but it would be necessary to let the rain rinse the salt off the sail before putting the water in the tank. Since squalls tend to be accompanied by strong winds and bouncy seas I am unsure if this method would work. Putting up an awning or special rain catcher in a squall would be an interesting and possibly fruitless exercise.

ANTIFOULING

Antifouling is about the last task before launching. Be generous and use several coats for it will have to work hard in warm tropical seas. This is the time to raise the boot-topping a few inches. Cruising yachts always sit low in the water. Just how low you discover by trial and error.

Parting with the cash for the refit marks the transition from up-market day-dreaming, which I dignify as planning, to hard-nosed preparation. Spending a small fortune can only be justified by an equal level of personal commitment. But before I could sail, and even as a single-hander, I had to look to the crew, their comfort and safety.

4 Choosing and Caring for the Crew

CHOOSING THE RIGHT CREW

Signing on the right crew for a transatlantic cruise is never easy. You are embarking on a great adventure; fulfilling the ambition of a lifetime and wishing it to be fun and memorable for the right reasons but, as William Bligh discovered, poor relations with your crew ruins the voyage for everyone.

There are four types of crew: single-handers, couples, friends, and families. Couples have been sailing the Atlantic for fun ever since Mr and Mrs Crapo sailed across in their 20-foot *New Bedford* in 1877. Some younger couples take a sabbatical year, some take the children, older couples have the time to join the international tribe of sea gipsies, and some, like me, sail alone and are joined by holidaying family and friends from time to time.

THE SINGLE-HANDER

Sailing single-handed evades the problems of choosing a crew but raises difficulties over watch keeping, sail handling and the question of who plays nurse if you fall ill. It would be wrong to make too much of the solitude that goes with solo sailing. An ocean voyage alone is so completely different from a short offshore passage that it is impossible to know if you can handle it until it is too late for second thoughts. The pros and cons of single-handed sailing is a debate that began before Joshua Slocum and its end is not in sight, but solo ocean passages have a long and honourable pedigree. Many of the great, pioneering voyages were small boat passages made by single-handers, but it is not for everyone and only you will know if it is for you.

SAILING WITH CHILDREN

Concerns for couples with young children are: 'How will the children react to being away from their relations, friends, school and places they know? What are the health and safety issues for children? And will their education suffer?' There are no simple or straightforward answers. Kids appear to profit from the experience. To me, they seem to benefit from having their parents around all the time. There are no latchkey kids at sea and despite having their parents always to hand they are independent, self-confident, and play their part in sailing and living aboard. Irrespective of language problems they mix well and make friends easily with children from other boats.

The usual childhood illnesses appear to raise no more problems than if they were living ashore. Watching the children swarm about the rigging dispels fears for their safety and they learn to swim like fish. It would appear the greatest danger is the usual range of bumps, scrapes and broken bones that children seem to attract as they grow up. I met one or two youngsters with an arm in plaster but no more than I would expect to meet ashore.

On the strength of a wholly unscientific survey, I reckon most liveaboard children are pre-teens. This may be because teenagers wish to spread their wings and prefer the company of their peers to their parents or because the teenage years are when schooling takes on an importance that reverberates throughout their life, and the family swallows the anchor until those years are out of the way.

SCHOOLING KIDS

Up to 11 or 12 years old, children may benefit from the widening of their horizons, seeing, instead of reading, about the world and people beyond their home town.

The subject of home schooling has generated a considerable amount of information, both on paper and the Internet, and distance learning and home schooling schemes are available to keep their formal education up with their stay-at-home contemporaries. *The Complete Home Schooling Source Book* by Rebecca Rupp, or *Home Schooling for Excellence* by David and Micki Colfax or *Home Schooling Handbook from Pre-School to High School: A Parents' Guide* may help. Or visit the Education Otherwise website. Other websites include www.netspace.org, which has details of educational on-line resources. The British government has its national curriculum and schemes of work on the Internet.

Distance learning schemes for children are available from the Calvert School, Maryland, USA or the World Educational Service in Britain. Calvert School, established in 1897, can provide a year's worth of textbooks, workbooks and lesson plans in a single package with free help a phone call or e-mail away. The World Educational Service started ten years earlier as the Parents' National Education Union. Its courses follow the British national curriculum but books and materials are extra.

A school visit before departure will help to find the most suitable learning programme and the rapid growth of Internet teaching packages might help. It may be possible to set up an Internet link with the school and keep in touch through the cruise. Internet teaching schemes with video conferencing already exist and some schools use them to provide tuition for small numbers of pupils in subjects where the school lacks a specialist teacher. This may be a partial answer for some families.

Home schooling, ashore or afloat, places heavy demands on parental time. There will be at least 12–15 hours a week actual teaching with almost as much time again spent in lesson preparation and marking which makes teaching the kids very nearly a full time job.

It may be a coincidence but most home schooling schemes stop when kids reach their thirteenth birthday. Teenage children need access to specialist tuition that not all parents can provide, even with help, and few yachts carry a science laboratory or a craft or electronics laboratory that some subjects require. On top of this there is always the threat of exams. A year out of school in the run up to exams may not be in their best interests.

Sailing as a family chooses your crew for you. With luck and good propaganda, blue-water cruising will be a family-wide ambition, and all that can be hoped is that the ups and downs of the voyage will be absorbed in the normal fluctuations of family life.

FRIENDS AS CREW

Cruising with friends makes onboard relationships both easier and harder. It is easier because, however inconvenient or difficult circumstances become, it is always possible to agree to differ, and go your separate ways. It is harder because friends will have contributed towards the running costs, helped prepare the yacht (what else are they for?), sought time off work or away from their family and made a huge emotional investment in the project. Friends will expect their views not just to be heard but also to be taken into account. It takes considerable maturity to accept that while everyone is sailing the dream, you may not share the

CREW MANAGEMENT

On long passages much of the skipper's day is taken up with the domestic rather than nautical elements of onboard life. He must decide who cooks, who washes up, and whose turn it is to clean the boat. If such mundane tasks are left to willing horses they quickly become a swamp for breeding resentment and arguments.

Draw up a daily sea routine before you leave port. Based on your watch system this will cover every minute of the day and make each watch responsible for their fair share of the daily chores. As the watches rotate then everyone has their dose of the good and the bad. The daily routine would lay down mealtimes, who is on standby watch, when the next watch is to be called and all the other trivia of daily life. Since food and water supplies are limited it can also include rules for their use. Finding someone has used several days' fresh water to rinse their laundry or devoured the last packet of chocolate biscuits can be hard to take especially if they justify their actions with 'You never said I couldn't.'

Once the daily routine has been discussed and agreed with the crew then commit it to paper and pin it up for all to see. This frees the skipper from becoming a nag, forever reminding people about what to do next. This improves his image because he is now able to assess relationships between crew members and step in early and light-handedly to defuse conflicts and disagreements long before they become critical, possibly even before the protagonists realise there is a problem.

DELEGATION

Everyone likes responsibility and making individual crew members responsible for specific tasks or areas of work is good but play to people's strengths and skills: make the car mechanic responsible for the engine, the maths professor the navigator, the radio ham the electrics. If they do not have the skills, try to provide training or reduce the tasks to a series of simple checks. Done well, delegation is a means of giving status, self-esteem and enhancing teamwork.

Once tasks have been delegated then let them get on with their job. Do not spend the day looking over shoulders telling people what to do and how to do it but have clear limits to their independence. Crew members must be in no doubt when to call the skipper and tell him what is happening. Besides the 'if in any doubt' clause in the standing orders simple trip wires are a good way of laying down limits. For the engineer this could be if the daily fuel consumption exceeded a laid down figure; for the navigator, an unduly large cross track error, or receiving a gale warning; for the watch officer seeing another vessel, changing course or sail plan. It helps to avoid misunderstanding if these duties and their limitations are written down.

Sea routines and delegation can evolve as a passage progresses until they fit like a well worn shoe but this can only happen if the skipper has put the groundwork in before sailing.

same dream. It does not matter that you have sailed together for years and are survivors of a thousand Channel passages. An Atlantic crossing is so different that it is a useless yardstick to compatibility.

If having friends for crew is fraught with difficulties then advertising for crew magnifies them tenfold. Who are these strangers? What are their backgrounds, their interests, moods, habits and temperaments? Are they into recreational drugs? This makes no moral judgement. If the authorities find drugs aboard it can mean losing your boat and as skipper some of the blame will

This is what you are aiming for: a boat-load of happy faces.

inevitably fall on you. Lots of people wish to sail across the Atlantic. At Las Palmas hopefuls leave copies of their CVs pinned anywhere they may be seen. Many have impressive sailing pedigrees but can you live with a stranger for four weeks? This sounds a silly question but a month can be no time at all or just short of the downside to eternity.

Modern society does not live in small, self-contained groups making their own entertainment, or travelling slowly. It hurries, journeying on land at 80mph and crossing the Atlantic in eight hours. 'Now' means yesterday and the 24/7 work ethic rules. On a good day, life at sea moves at a brisk walk even if the mind is still travelling at 80mph. Some days there is no progress. There are no films or TV and never any escape from the same faces, voices, ticks and quirks. With nothing better to think about, small mannerisms blister otherwise placid temperaments. Slights fester, tempers flare, arguments erupt, and black spots are exchanged.

Crews have arrived in the Caribbean with the skipper issuing helm orders through his solicitor, and devoted couples close to or beyond divorce. I met an American yacht where the owners, a long-married couple, refereed by their paid, professional skipper, battled like cold war superpowers over the finer points of a simple overnight passage towards the Caribbean. They made that passage but never reached the Caribbean. Enforced proximity leavened with uncertainty can be fatal to any relationship and there is no formula that says which mix of personalities will be the best recipe for a harmonious trip.

If you decide to advertise for crew, then a short familiarisation cruise as part of the interview may reveal the unsuitable applicants but is not necessarily a sure guide to compatibility for it is much harder to put your best face forward for three or four weeks than for three or four days.

If you are confident of your yacht-handling ability then rate crew compatibility far above competent crew. If, before you are committed to making the transatlantic crossing, there is a hint of incompatibility

between you and any of your crew then look for ways to part as friends without either side losing face. Folk can be taught how to sail as they go but people cannot be taught how to live together in harmony.

THE RESPONSIBLE SKIPPER

Even if you are living in a state of undeclared war with your crew, do not overlook the fact that as long as they are on the ship's papers each and every one of them remains the skipper's responsibility. This is usually unimportant in home waters but further afield these responsibilities become very real and breaches carry heavy financial penalties. Immigration officers, for example, demand assurances that you will take your crew with you when you leave. The only acceptable excuses are crew members leaving to join another yacht (much paperwork is needed to prove this) or that as they sign off your boat they produce a ticket home. If they fall ill you may have to pay their medical bills, and until they leave, you are expected to cover their living costs.

Nit-picking or not, it is wise to insist that everyone on board has had their prophylactic jabs. Check that no one is suffering from any chronic illness or on medication and everyone holds a valid, comprehensive medical insurance policy good for several million pounds sterling (or its equivalent), including medical repatriation home. If they are making a one-way trip they must have either a ticket home or the cash to buy one and insist that everyone hands over documentary evidence in the form of tickets, cash, insurance certificates and passports to the skipper for their safe keeping and his peace of mind.

HEALTH MATTERS

Much of what I read either suggested that I was about to visit the Islands of Doctor Moreau or that my appendix was primed to blow up in the middle of the ocean, but if you start out fit and well then with a few common sense precautions you will probably stay healthy.

IMMUNISATIONS

Some immunisations take time to become effective so about two months before departure everyone must discuss the voyage with their doctor and seek advice about how the trip may affect their health together with any particular precautions they should take. This is especially important if they have a pre-existing medical condition.

RECIPROCAL HEALTH AGREEMENTS

Nationals of the European Economic Area (the EEA comprises the members of the EU plus Iceland, Liechtenstein and Norway) can obtain free or reduced cost health care inside the EEA. In the UK this is obtained by going to a post office and completing Form E111. The UK has reciprocal health care agreements with Anguilla, Barbados, British Virgin Islands, Monserrat, and the Turks and Caicos Islands.

SOURCES OF ADVICE ON HEALTH

Specialist advice on particular risks can be obtained from organisations such as MATSA (UK) or Centers for Disease Control (USA). Both have websites. Other UK based helplines are found at the Hospital for Tropical Diseases (0839 337733) and the Malaria Healthline (0891 600350). These are both premium rate telephone numbers. If you choose to obtain medical advice via the Internet choose reputable sites that give

---

ORAL REHYDRATION SALTS

Most deaths from diarrhoea are from dehydration. This is the loss of water and salts from the body. Oral Rehydration Therapy (ORT) replaces fluids and salts lost through diarrhoea. If fluid intake is increased as soon as diarrhoea starts it is reckoned that around 90% of acute diarrhoea cases can be treated successfully at home or on board.

Oral Rehydration Salts (ORS) approved by the World Health Organisation and UNICEF contain:

- 3.5g sodium chloride
- 1.5g potassium chloride
- 2.9g trisodium citrate
- 20g anhydrous glucose.

This comes as a powder in a standard packet whose contents are dissolved in one litre of water. Packets that use bicarbonate of soda (2.5g) instead of trisodium citrate are acceptable but cannot be stored for very long.

Sugar-salt solution (SSS) is a home made version of ORS containing 3 grams (half a level standard 5ml teaspoon) of salt, 18 grams (4 teaspoons) of sugar and dissolved in one litre of water. This can be made up from salt and sugar on board as required.

As a guide, the amount of ORS or SSS given should be:

- A child under two years old should be given about 50–100ml ($1/_4$–$1/_2$ cup) of rehydration fluid after each loose stool.
- Older children will require 100–200ml ($1/_2$–1 cup) after each loose stool.
- Children over ten years old and adults can drink as much as they want.

Other good fluids include yoghurt drinks, water in which a cereal (such as rice) has been cooked, unsweetened tea, green coconut water and unsweetened, fresh fruit juice. Avoid fizzy drinks or drinks containing stimulants such as caffeine.

Drinking ORS solution is not a cure. It prevents dehydration. It does not stop the diarrhoea and if the diarrhoea persists medical advice should be sought.

information written or checked by named, qualified professionals. Visit more than one site and be cautious of accepting information provided by commercially sponsored sites; if in any doubt check out your findings with your doctor.

HEALTH RISKS ON BOARD

Health risks differ depending on whether you are at sea or ashore. At sea falling ill is always a worry but if you are healthy when you leave port then the greatest health risks are from traumatic injuries like strains, slips, falls, scalds and cuts. With the possible exceptions of toothache or food poisoning either from careless preparation or eating that last morsel of dodgy ham, bugs are scarce at sea. Food poisoning is more likely ashore and it is wise to avoid eating in that delightful ethnic restaurant on the night before departure.

SHORESIDE HEALTH RISKS

No one is counting but road traffic accidents and violent muggings almost certainly head the list of shoreside health risks. The tropics also have a number of exotic dangers to your health carried by insects, in food and water or from person to person. They sound scary but, although there must be a few cases every season, most folk take sensible precautions and stay healthy. The most important precautions are to always treat drinking and cooking water, keep the galley clean and watch what you eat. If you go snorkelling or diving, look but do not touch for some underwater inhabitants might object and if you wish to wander along jungle paths wear sensible shoes and clothing and watch out for the occasional sunbathing snake.

Medical facilities in major population centres range from adequate to good but even the best possibly lack specialised resources and equipment. In more remote areas, medical provision is likely to be a visiting nurse or a doctor holding a weekly or monthly clinic. Far off the beaten track, the position is exactly the same as if on passage: you are on your own until you reach civilisation.

FIRST AID

At least one person, and preferably everyone, should hold a recognised, current first aid certificate and it is advisable for one crew member to attend the more advanced Ship's Captain's Medical Course.

It takes at least six years' hard work to qualify as a doctor. Boy scouts carrying out heart transplants using a Swiss army knife and a sticking plaster make a good tale but unless there is a doctor on board, therapy is unlikely to go much beyond treating casualties for shock, immobilising injuries, avoiding or reducing infection and controlling pain. This is where the time spent before you sail making sure that the cabin is warm and dry, the bunks are comfortable, and the boat rigged for short-handed sailing (you are now a crew member short) pays off. The best place for the sick, including the seasick and wounded, is a comfortable and secure bunk.

Unless moaning makes you feel better, afflictions like toothache are best dealt with by suffering quietly. Having once finished Denmark's Round Zealand Race with a cartoon-like swollen face and existing on nicotine and schnapps I know that toothache at sea is a visit to purgatory, but amateur tooth pulling is very risky. When I got ashore the dentist's first action was to put me on a two-week course of antibiotics to control the infection, followed by a couple of weeks of drilling and filling. Your first aid kit should include a good stock of broad spectrum antibiotics (check if any of your crew are allergic to penicillin) and strong pain killers so that infections can be contained and pain controlled until proper medical assistance is reached.

SAFETY ON BOARD

True safety has more to do with attitude than equipment. Being aware of risks is more important than the mindless compliance with routine safety measures. It is easy to concentrate on the dramatic, ultimate disaster but this can hide the real risks; truly great

THE MEDICAL BOX

This should contain the following:

Analgesics; antibiotics; antimalarial pills; antiseptic solutions and creams; preparations for allergic reactions, eye and ear disorders, gastro-intestinal disorders, seasickness, skin problems and allergies.

It is important that you are absolutely clear about:

- the illness each medicine can treat
- the dosage to be given and if it differs for children and adults or pregnant women
- the side effects
- how it is administered and for how long
- how it interacts with other drugs
- how it should be stored
- its shelf life. Most will come marked with its batch number and expiry date but this may be missing on some dispensed items.
- who is included in the risk groups. Children and the elderly? Pregnant women?

These details for each medicine should be written down and kept on laminated sheets in the medicine box. This goes beyond the usual advice of 'take three times daily after meals' and the surest way of finding this information is to discuss your requirements with your doctor.

He can also provide a list of recommended medicines and prescriptions where necessary. Do not forget to ask him for a letter which will act as certification that you are carrying these drugs for medical purposes. This is to satisfy curious customs officers, and as some may become out of date during your cruise ask for a repeat prescription so that you can obtain replacements for controlled drugs and those available only on prescription.

EQUIPMENT AND DRESSINGS

If you are not already carrying the following items in your first aid box consider adding them before you sail.

Steristrips
Crepe bandages (10cm)
Crepe bandages (5cm)
Gauze swabs
Jelonet
Needle packs
Brook airway
Surgical scissors
Toothfil dental kit
Mediswabs
Zinc oxide tape
Clinical thermometer
Stethoscope
Sphygmomanometer (for blood pressure)
Sticking plasters various sizes
Sticking plaster rolls various
Inflatable splints
Adhesive elastoplast bandages
Wound dressings

Apart from the main medical box it would be useful to have two smaller first aid kits: one easily to hand for the day-to-day minor scrapes and the other available for the crash box in case you have to abandon ship.

disasters come not from a single cause, but from an unholy alliance of insignificant trivia massing together at the wrong time in the right place to overwhelm you.

I gave priority to making sure that I could move around *Mintaka* and *Margo* in any weather without being injured. In practice this amounts to being able to hang on or being wedged in place. On *Mintaka* this was easy. In the cabin I either sat, or lay down. In each position I was immovable and if I opened the main hatch and stood up I was jammed in the hatch and able to handle both main and jib without leaving the cabin or taking out the washboards. Had I wished, I could have spent the entire crossing in the cabin and never gone on deck.

On *Margo* I could stand up and move around below decks so I fitted extra grab handles in the cabin, but not enough, and once or twice took painful falls – a reminder to fit more grab handles. A liberal application of an aggressive non-slip paint to the deck and easy-to-use grabrails made going forward from the cockpit sure footed if not safe and I could handle every sail, except the cruising chute, from the cockpit.

GOING WALKABOUT

Staying aboard when underway is important. Miracles excepted, a single-hander going overboard is dead. In all likelihood, this is true of anyone falling over the side, particularly at night or in heavy weather. Lifejackets will keep them afloat, the MOB button on the GPS and electronic homing devices, lights and markers will guide a vessel back to whoever is in the water. Even so there are cases where crew have fallen overboard in daylight and have been lost. Technology is wonderful, not infallible. If someone is in the water it is far better that they are dragged alongside by their harness and bang on the hull until someone answers than being left astern to be found later.

Anyone falling overboard and becoming separated from the yacht should not attempt to swim, a pointless activity in mid-ocean, but to conserve body warmth and energy by adopting the HELP position (Fig 8 page 52).

Attached to the boat the casualty still needs to climb back aboard. This is not always easy. If there is not a boarding ladder at the stern then it ought to be possible to clamber up the self-steering gear. On *Mintaka* I carried rope boarding ladders on either side of the cockpit that I could pull down and climb up, and on *Margo* I also tied a couple of loops in short lengths of rope and lashed them at intervals along the coachroof grabrail to do the same job. The idea was that I would always have some sort of rope ladder within reach. Once I had my weight on my

feet I reckoned I could scramble inboard and I always managed it in practice.

I have never had to bring an unconscious or helpless crew member aboard but, apart from proprietary recovery systems, both halyards and mainsheets can be used to beef up muscle power.

ANCHOR POINTS FOR HARNESSES

On both *Margo* and *Mintaka* anchor points for harnesses are spaced so that I clip in before opening the hatch, and by using two safety lines, never unclip until I am back in the cabin and the hatch shut. Ian on *Timna* had safety lines permanently attached to the jackstays running fore and aft either side of the cockpit. No more leaning over the guardrails to clip in and no more wondering if the snapshackle will snag. A splendid example which I had no hesitation in following.

All this is a counsel of perfection and there are times I romp around the cockpit without wearing a harness. I only have myself to please (and blame) but when there are others aboard I insist harnesses are worn and used all of the time. I know this is hypocritical but if the crew complain about me infringing their human rights I sling an empty can over the side, count to five and ask them how long they would take to sail back and pick it up. In the Trades with boomed-out headsails the correct answer is, 'forever'.

CLIMBING THE MAST

After the perils of falling overboard, climbing the mast at sea comes next in my catalogue of fears. I have a rock climber's dislike of hanging on a rope. So far, installing extra halyards and spare navigation lights during the pre-cruise refit has made mast-climbing at sea unnecessary and the job of replacing halyards or burnt out bulbs waits until I am at anchor.

For mast climbing I wear a climbing harness left over from my more adventurous days and use ascendeurs. Climbing harnesses are far superior to bosun's chairs. They are

Ascendeurs are a reasonably safe and comfortable way of climbing up the mast to carry out repairs.

more comfortable and you can hang upside down in a climbing harness and not fall out. Using ascendeurs (sometimes called cloggers or jumars) there is no need for someone to tail a winch. Ascendeurs come in pairs; one is attached to the harness at waist level and the other to a loop of rope that acts as a stirrup. They go on separate halyards for safety and pushing them up alternately I make a slow, stately and safe ascent. A short safety line goes from the harness to a third halyard and is fastened with a prussick knot that slides up as I go, and if all else fails this will catch me.

THE CAPTAIN'S ROUNDS

The daily captain's rounds have as much to do with safety as they have with maintenance. I start aft and work forward up the port side and back along the starboard side. I check the self-steering gear, the rudder, the tiller, and every shroud and bottlescrew. I make sure that the sails are not chafing and the sheets and halyards are running free. I inspect every sheet and halyard for chafe, delve into cockpit lockers to check that the gas bottles and piping are in good condition and secure. Gas alarms are great but a visual check is better. I give the batteries their health check, dip the fuel tank and ensure the fuel cans are secure and not leaking. The water tank is inspected, the fresh fruit and vegetables examined and the ready-to-use food stores restocked. Every hull fitting is checked and every seacock turned on and off. Floorboards are raised to expose the bilges which are pumped to prove the pump is working. Every boat should have at least two hand pumps of a size that allows a frightened man to throw several hundred gallons a minute overboard. One, at least, should be in the cabin and usable with the cabin secured against bad weather.

To carry out these simple checks properly demands a level of self-discipline I do not always display. Heavy weather, for example, can see them disappear entirely from the agenda but they are important. A stitch in time saves nine is trite but very true. Inspections and the day-to-day maintenance that follows reduces the likelihood of an incident occurring, but should a problem arise I know my boat's condition without wasting time finding out.

Every ship should have its daily walkabout routine. With a crew, the work of checking the boat can be shared out. This will speed the process and if the results are logged a full history will be instantly available if needed.

PROBLEM SOLVING

Like unwanted guests problems arrive unexpectedly and, despite well mannered hints, are reluctant to depart. At sea they will either sink the boat or they will not.

When it is certain that the boat is lost then the only course of action is an orderly departure, which brings everyone safely ashore. When making the decision to abandon ship there is no time to think about

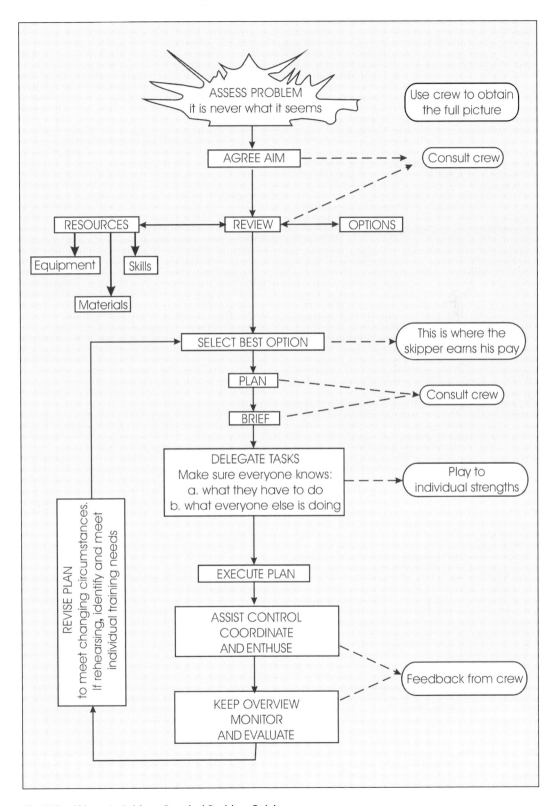

Fig 6 *The Skipper's Guide to Practical Problem Solving.*

how it should be implemented. Every minute, every second, should be spent executing a carefully thought out, well rehearsed plan in which everyone knows what they have to do and does it.

Events are unlikely to go according to plan but this is not an excuse for playing them off the cuff. It is far better to vary a plan than to make it up as you go along. You must decide your priorities and allocate resources accordingly.

Different ships, different cap tallies but whatever plan you finally settle upon put the theory to test and rehearse it a couple of times with your crew to iron out any snags and to make sure everyone knows what to do.

As part of their planning, skippers should consider how they will convince their crew that in the absence of a perfect solution (several will appear with hindsight) then a less than perfect answer enthusiastically implemented by the crew working as a team is far better than everyone sitting down and discussing what makes the ideal answer.

Other problems range from the trivial, such as loss of engine or battery power, to the more serious such as losing a mast, or above-waterline damage or the rudder falling off. In inshore waters, the time available to resolve such difficulties is determined by how long it will take you to hit the rocks but far out at sea it is very different. Outside help may be longer coming but in every case, once the situation is contained and the risk of further damage or loss reduced, there is time to sit down, have a cup of tea and think the problem through. I have met minor problems a couple of times and on the one occasion I did not take time to think, I made matters worse.

SURVIVAL AT SEA

The possibility of losing the boat and its aftermath has always been the focus of attention. Studying reports of sinkings in World War Two, Alain Bombard, a French doctor, was struck by the fact that many crews successfully abandoned ship but died soon afterwards even though they were uninjured and were in tropical waters where hypothermia was not a factor. Bombard concluded that they died because they did not expect to live. He came to believe that survival for long periods was possible and cited the example of Second Steward Poon Lim of the SS *Ben Lomond* which was torpedoed and sank on 23 November 1942; Lim was rescued alive 133 days later.

Taking Lim's experience a step further Bombard argued that it was possible to survive at sea even if you had no food or water. In 1952 he proved his theory by successfully sailing a 15-foot inflatable called *l'Heritique* from France to Barbados, including a 65-day non-stop passage from Las Palmas to Barbados. Apart from one light meal from a passing ship he ate and drank only what he got from the sea. His extraordinary example must have helped folk like the Baileys (118 days adrift), and the Robertsons (84 days adrift).

GMDSS, particularly the 406MHz EPIRB, makes it unlikely that these incidents will be repeated, but what if the EPIRB fails? Impossible? What would happen if a lightning strike blew out every seacock and sank the boat? Lightning kills electrics, including EPIRBs. Even a near miss will make an EPIRB very sick and Murphy's Law of the Sea has a paragraph on other circumstances, as yet unknown, where EPIRBs will fail.

LIFEBOAT VERSUS LIFE RAFT

I carry an EPIRB and I will use it if I have to but I also plan to survive, if I can or have to, by my own efforts. This took me into the thick of the life raft versus lifeboat debate. Life rafts are compact, easy to stow, and quick to launch but once you are inside you are a passive victim of the winds and currents. This is acceptable in busy coastal or offshore waters where rescue can be expected in hours rather than days, but stories of those who had to leave their yachts in mid-ocean convinced me that if they had been able to spend a fraction of the ingenuity and determination they devoted to surviving into sailing in the

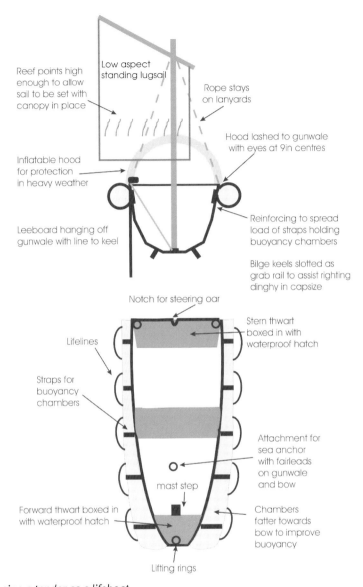

Reef points high
enough to allow
sail to be set with
canopy in place

Low aspect
standing lugsail

Rope stays
on lanyards

Hood lashed to gunwale
with eyes at 9in centres

Inflatable hood
for protection
in heavy weather

Leeboard hanging off
gunwale with line to keel

Reinforcing to spread
load of straps holding
buoyancy chambers

Bilge keels slotted as
grab rail to assist righting
dinghy in capsize

Notch for steering oar

Stern thwart
boxed in with
waterproof hatch

Lifelines

Straps for
buoyancy
chambers

Attachment for
sea anchor
with fairleads
on gunwale
and bow

mast step

Forward thwart boxed in
with waterproof hatch

Chambers
fatter towards
bow to improve
buoyancy

Lifting rings

Fig 7 *Ideas for using a tender as a lifeboat.*

direction of their choice they would have reached safety much sooner. What they needed was a lifeboat not a life raft, a conclusion that the Robertsons reached the hard way when they abandoned their life raft and took to their dinghy in the hope of reaching land.

Very few yachts have the space to carry a lifeboat even if it does double duty as a tender. Also a lifeboat takes longer to launch and is more vulnerable than a life raft in heavy

weather but in reasonable conditions it could make 40 or 50 miles a day.

This reasoning became the basis of my worse case scenario planning but locating a lifeboat that would fit on a 20-foot yacht proved a challenge. All I could find was a Tinker Tramp. This is an inflatable dinghy with a folding, hard wooden floor and can be rigged for sailing or given an inflatable hood to become a life raft. Even though air bottles can be fitted to inflate it quickly, in an

The Tinker Tramp makes a good tender and fun boat in harbour; when not in use the Tramp lives (very well secured) before the mast.

emergency it would still take longer to launch than a life raft, and deflated and rolled up it is bulkier than both a conventional inflatable dinghy and a life raft. A big plus is that unlike a conventional life raft it is possible to check its condition frequently, practise using it in its various modes and have confidence that if it is needed it will work. They are not cheap and the argument that they cost little more than the combined cost of a rubber dinghy and a life raft fell down for me because, like most people, I had a perfectly good inflatable dinghy. A Tinker Tramp may not be ideal but the market is not brimming with choice.

I bought one, took it sailing on a wet, windy Easter day, promptly capsized and discovered that, soaked and wearing oilskins, boarding a Tinker Tramp is not easy. It did not help that other Tinker Tramps sailed by crying, 'We've never seen one of these capsize before.' Whilst dog paddling shorewards towing the Tinker Tramp behind me, I made a mental note to carry a boarding ladder. Once accustomed to its quirks, the Bermudan rig gave a surprisingly good performance but I am not sure it is best for its role as a lifeboat where most travelling will be downwind and down current, and performance is less important. Perhaps a simple, easily-rigged standing lug would be better.

THE CRASH BOX

Taking to a life raft or lifeboat is only a start. Now you must stay alive. The crash box ought to hold all you need to stay alive. It must be robust to withstand the inevitable abuse, hold its contents securely, be waterproof, buoyant, easily recognisable by night or day and have a foolproof and secure method of attachment to the life raft.

I use large, plastic flare boxes. They are liberally covered in photo-luminescent tape that glows in the dark. This was intended to make them easy to find in the forepeak at night but in future I would also attach a small, waterproof, battery operated strobe to make sure that if I had to abandon ship at night then the odds on losing sight of the crash box if it went adrift were much reduced.

In daylight, a high-visibility orange flare box would be better than my grey boxes. Each box, I had two, has a line spliced to its handle with a snaplink at its free end. Everything I planned to take into the life raft had the same arrangement of line and snaplink. I can tie bowlines in the dark, behind my back and underwater but I know the time I'll make a mistake is when it really counts. Clipping the snaplinks to the grab line round the Tinker reduces the possibility of anything going adrift even in a capsize.

Hard plastic boxes protect their contents but some people prefer a soft crash bag as it is easier to stow in odd shaped lockers until it is needed. The comments about the importance of visibility, security and flotation still apply with the rider that the contents must be individually protected against abuse. To improve visibility and flotation it might help to lash the crash bag into a lifejacket equipped with its own strobe light.

In another crash box I packed the ship's papers, my passport, some cash (in dollars) and credit cards. I also included a notebook and pencil and filled the spare space with food. This is the secondary box, the one I would take with me if I were taken off by another vessel or open when I reached land.

Emergency rations

The priorities for survival are shelter, water and food. The canopy of a life raft or the Tinker Tramp would provide shelter but I also carried a heavy-duty exposure suit. I could not find solar stills to distil fresh water from sea water and I could not afford a small, hand-operated water maker so I would have to carry my water with me and hope to supplement it from passing rain showers. Alain Bombard claimed it is possible to drink up to half a pint of sea-water a day provided you started immediately you entered the life raft, before you became dehydrated. This is an extreme view. He survived, but I am not sure I would have the same degree of confidence in this practice. As a supplement to the canned water in the crashbox I carried two 5-gallon (18-litre) plastic water jugs in the cockpit.

Each held between 4 and 4½ gallons (15 to 17 litres) to make sure that they would float. This represented about 20 days of water.

I carried as many cans of food as I could squeeze into the crash box, trying to avoid products high in thirst-inducing salt (it is surprising how high salt comes on the list of the ingredients on many cans) and gave preference to food high in fluids. Canned fruit is good. I also included sugary snacks as quick energy and morale boosters. If time allowed then the ready-to-use food (about a week's worth of food at normal consumption stored in a plastic box) would be taken into the life raft.

I have serious doubts about my ability to live off the sea. I am an inept fisherman. I've trolled a line for thousands of miles but I can only recall two occasions when fish deigned to bite. Both woke up quickly, realised their mistake and escaped. In the hope that necessity would be a better teacher than boredom I included fishing lines, with lots of hooks and lures and a chopping board and knife to prepare any fish foolish enough to fall for my tricks.

ATTRACTING ATTENTION

I assume that I would have to bring my predicament to the attention of other vessels. As well as a 406MHz EPIRB I carry flares, smoke, signal mirrors and strobes but have heard too many tales of flares burning unseen to have much faith in them as the principal means of attracting notice.

I like the idea of the Skystreme. This is an inflatable, radar reflective kite, which packs away to the size of a credit card, weighs 43 grams and can be flown in winds from under four knots to a force 10. It flies at heights of up to 100 feet (30 metres) saying, 'Here I am' 24 hours a day.

My principal means of calling for help is a handheld VHF radio. Ships, even far from land, tend to keep a watch on channel 16 and once I had their attention I could use flares, smoke and strobes to indicate my position. I am not certain how this will work when GMDSS comes into full force and ships no

longer stand watch on channel 16. Although they are expensive, GMDSS-compatible handheld VHF radios are now coming onto the market and will make a Mayday call automatically. I put a handheld VHF radio with a spare battery into the crash box and one of my regular chores was to make sure that both were fully charged.

GOING ALONGSIDE AT SEA

Asking a passing ship for a few gallons of fuel or water may seem to be the solution to an unexpected shortage but be careful. Going alongside a larger vessel at sea can fatally damage your boat. To avoid being sucked into the larger vessel stay outside the equilateral triangle whose sides are equal to the length of the larger vessel. If you must go alongside to collect supplies or deliver an injured crew member then consider using the dinghy. Without a yardstick to give scale, distances off are hard to judge. Ships are often bigger and further away than they look. If you do not have a radar set then ask them for the distance off.

ABANDONING SHIP

I had a routine worked out: first launch the Tinker, then the primary crash box, followed by the 5-gallon (18-litre) water containers, next the ready-to-use food box and finally the secondary crash box together with anything else I could lay hands on.

My plan allowed for four or five days spent close to where I abandoned ship to see if the EPIRB brought a result. If it did not then I would continue on my way. To navigate the Tinker Tramp across the ocean, to the primary crash box I added a handheld GPS programmed with a selection of likely waypoints, a compass, and a small laminated chart of the Atlantic Ocean showing the principal shipping lanes, a torch and spare batteries.

If you need help then it may be several days before it arrives and is most likely to come from a vessel taking part in the AMVER (Automated Mutual Vessel Rescue)

EMERGENCY ANTENNA

In an emergency, a usable half-wave dipole antenna can be made from the remnants of your old aerial which is useful if you have broken the mast and cut the top half with the antenna away.

Start with a suitable length of coaxial cable. The old cable will do. If you are thinking of buying spare cable then it will most probably have an impedance of either 50 or 75 ohms. Check in your radio's instruction manual. Strip about 20in (500mm) of the outer sheath to expose the braid.

Carefully feed the inner core through the braid where it leaves the outer sheath. Trim both the inner core and the braid so that they are exactly 17.5in (445mm) long. Lay out the inner core and the braid so that they form one straight line and tape to a sail batten.

Plug the other end of the cable into your radio and hang the antenna as high as possible so that the batten is vertical and you have a VHF half-wave dipole antenna. It has no gain but it should give reasonable performance.

More elaborate models can be made using small-diameter copper tubing but this version has the advantage that it can be made with the materials most likely to be at hand.

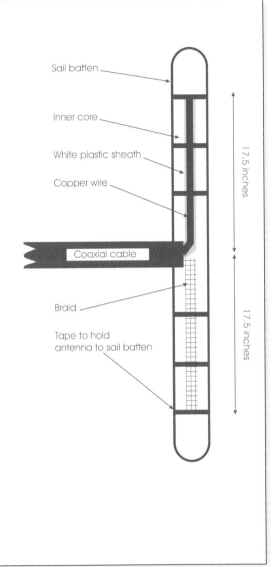

Sail batten

Inner core

White plastic sheath

Copper wire

Coaxial cable

Braid

Tape to hold antenna to sail batten

17.5 inches

17.5 inches

scheme which tracks vessels taking part so that the nearest can be diverted to give assistance in an emergency. When it does arrive on scene the priority is to save the crew. Salvage, if it figures at all, will be far down the list and even if willing, few commercial vessels have the equipment or expertise to lift a yacht safely out of the water at sea. Also it will be very difficult and dangerous to lower the mast before the yacht is taken aboard. Asking for help means the situation is so serious that you are willing to trade your boat, its equipment and most of its contents for the safety of you and your crew.

If there is no immediate danger of foundering, then this becomes what politicians call a hard choice. A Swiss yacht was becalmed with its engine broken beyond onboard repair north of St Martin. Hurricane Lenny, a Category 4 monster, was expected to pass over them, either that day, or perhaps the day after. In any event, they did not

Body heat is lost 25 times faster in water
than in air at the same temperature.
The HELP (Heat Escape Lessening Position)
can reduce heat loss by up to 50 per cent.

SIGNS OF HYPOTHERMIA

- Shivering
- Numbness
- Weakness
- Impaired vision
- Confusion
- Impaired judgement
- Dizziness

STAGES OF HYPOTHERMIA

1 Shivering
2 Apathy
3 Loss of consciousness
4 Slowing heart beat and breathing
5 Death

Fig 8 *Reducing body heat loss in an emergency.*

expect to sail out of Lenny's path. The crew put out a Mayday and were taken off and the yacht was abandoned. Lenny reached St Martin, stopped and turned south. It would never have reached them and the abandoned yacht was eventually found by fishermen and towed, more or less undamaged, into Great Inagau in the Bahamas.

On paper it looked as if my dues to safety had been paid. As usual everything was heavy on theory and second-hand opinion. When I met my first serious blow north of the Cape Verde Islands, the notion of leaving *Mintaka* and taking to those seas in the Tinker Tramp filled me with horror. A yacht is definitely the best life raft you can have.

5 The First Leg: Portugal, Madeira and Atlantic Islands

As departure approached I had many moments if not of dread then certainly of doubt. This was unexpected. A few months earlier I would have sailed without a second thought. I had faith in the work I had done on *Mintaka*. There were no worries about either vessel's seaworthiness. I had no qualms about my skills but I remained uneasy about sailing. As my sailing date neared, my unease grew stronger. I told myself it was a form of nautical stage fright and I would be all right on the night. After all it was my first Atlantic crossing and I had no idea what lay ahead. Teetering on the edge of my doubts I wondered if it had been the same for others. What had Mrs Slocum said to Joshua? My wife Liz saw through my doubts more clearly than me. 'Go and see how far you get,' she said, adding, 'If you don't go then you'll never know.' She was right and so I went to sea and it rained.

It was May and rain was falling in Tees Bay on the north east coast of England. Chilled by a blustery northeaster, fresh from the Arctic, the rain peppered the sea bringing visibility down to yards, leaving *Mintaka* and me in a small world of our own. Cold and wet I struggled with the Navik self-steering. Until it was persuaded to work for a living I could not reef the main and until that was done and *Mintaka* declared herself happy, I could not go below and change. Nothing was going according to plan.

It was my first passage of the season and I felt unready for sea. I was not even wearing oilskins. The simplest of tasks took far too long. The temptation to turn tail was nearly irresistible. 'There's no disgrace in going back,' I told myself but I knew that once inside the marina, excuses for delay would flourish and multiply. The Navik relented and slotted into place. The reef rattled into the main; the jib rolled away. At last *Mintaka* was behaving herself and pointing in the general direction of Whitby. Drenched to the skin, I dived into the chaos that was the cabin to hunt up warm, dry clothing. In an effort to bolster my spirits I kept telling myself that it would all seem different with a few miles under the keel, but when I hurried back into the cockpit I found that in my absence the rain had turned to sleet. What joy.

SHAKE-DOWN CRUISE

This trip round the coast to Falmouth was invaluable as a shake-down cruise. To cast off and blithely sail away into the blue without sea trials is an act of folly. I could more or less get away with it in *Mintaka* for I had made no changes of any importance and I knew her ways. Problems were mere niggles. The faulty compass light was traced to dodgy wiring. The autohelm's reluctance to work was caused by water upsetting its electronic digestion and cured by experts in Lowestoft. Running towards Brighton, the spinnaker pole went walkabout when a fitting parted company with the mast and provided a

WINDS

Winter gales and the hurricane season will determine your timings but the Westerlies, the north-east Trades and the Horse Latitudes are the winds that rule an Atlantic Circuit and dominate your route planning.

THE HADLEY CELL

Warm air at the equator rises, causing a low pressure area to form roughly 5° north and south of the equator. This is the Doldrums. When the air reaches an altitude where it is at the same temperature and density as the surrounding air it heads north (in the northern hemisphere), cooling as it goes until it sinks back to earth creating a high pressure area on the surface around 30° latitude. As it sinks the air becomes warmer and holds more moisture, giving clear skies and little rainfall. When it reaches the surface, air from the high pressure area travels south to the equatorial low pressure area. This movement of air produces a closed cell called a Hadley cell after George Hadley who was the first to work it out in 1735.

THE CORIOLIS EFFECT

Due to the Coriolis effect, winds in the Northern hemisphere are deflected to the right and so the winds blowing towards the equator from the high pressure area at 30°N do not blow from north to south but from north-east to south-west. This had been known for centuries but the explanation had to wait until 1835 when Gaspard Gustave de Coriolis discovered that the earth's daily rotation deflects all free moving objects to the right in the northern hemisphere and to the left in the southern hemisphere. Since the equatorial Hadley cell is very stable, these winds are persistent and steady in their direction. They are the north-east Trades.

THE WESTERLIES

There is a second Hadley cell between 30° and 60° north and here the Coriolis effect means that the surface winds blow from the south-west to the north-east and are called the Westerlies. In the northern hemisphere weather generated by the seasonal heating and cooling of the continents (Africa, the Americas and Europe) disturbs the Westerlies so that their regularity cannot match that of the north-east Trades. It is salutary to remember that in the southern hemisphere where these winds are not so affected by land masses they are, with good reason, called the Roaring Forties.

Between the Westerlies and the north-east Trades is a belt of calms and light, variable winds called the Horse Latitudes.

moment's excitement while I tamed the spinnaker – which took full advantage of its unexpected freedom. Putting these defects and a hundred other minor niggles right meant that by the time Falmouth was reached, *Mintaka* was fighting fit for sea.

It was not so with *Margo* when I set out on my second Atlantic circuit. Even when we reached Falmouth we were still strangers learning each other's ways. Refitting delays brought my timetable dangerously close to being stuck at home for another year and I justified a rushed departure and a dash round the coast on the grounds that waiting for perfection meant never sailing.

This was foolish but fortunately the faults were minor: the galley was not right; the sink was useless; the fresh water pump horribly slow and difficult to use; there were not enough grab handles below; care was needed using the steps to the cockpit in bouncy weather; these were all points that a season's cruising would have revealed and another winter's refit put right.

It would not have solved the riddle of the perfect stowage system. Every ocean cruiser has twice as much kit as locker space. Entire cabins have circled the Atlantic filled with equipment waiting to be stowed 'one day'. The ideal solution is to throw half the kit away and stow everything else by numbers but I have not yet met anyone that organised. Give some thought to stowage before you sail.

Try fitting doors to those open trough lockers that line the inside of the hull on many yachts. Not only will this prevent their contents flying around the cabin but also they will hold more and make the cabin look tidier. Do not stow anything in the bilges you are not prepared to see soaked and for the same reason items stowed in lockers under bunks should be protected against wet. You will have lots of charts. Roll them up and stow in lengths of plastic drain pipe bought from your local builders' merchant. At the same time buy caps to go over the ends of each length so your charts are safe from damp. Break up large lockers with plastic boxes of the type found in most DIY stores. They come in different sizes and colours that can be used to colour code their contents. Fit netting to deckheads. If you do not use nets for stowing fruit and vegetables they are good for keeping odds and ends out of the way. Think about classifying stowage as ready to use, to hand (eventually) and deep, long term stowage.

Changing your mind might be seen as failure and difficult to do if you have a crew to disappoint but you will never know unless you ask. Draw up a list of key ports, like Falmouth, where everyone can sit down, sup a pint, say their piece and agree where to go next. If nothing else, knowing plans can change takes the pressure off individuals and breaking the cruise into small, easily digested pieces concentrates minds on achievable immediate goals rather than distant dreams. Compared to 3000 miles over the Atlantic, the 400 miles across the Bay of Biscay is a mere bagatelle.

A key port is one where you choose between a long committing passage towards the Caribbean and a range of shorter passages that take you in other directions. Falmouth is a good example. Even the decision to continue towards the Caribbean has its choices. You can make directly across the Bay of Biscay for La Coruña, leapfrog to Spain via Brittany and the Basque Country or hop over to the south coast of Ireland before dropping down to La Coruña.

The menu of shorter passages includes making for the Mediterranean sun via the French canals. Why not spend a season or two cruising in the Mediterranean and then decide where to go next? Or hug the French coast with a detour through the Channel Islands? Even if the decision is to go home then the return passage can be a lazy cruise zigzagging up the Channel or sailing up the west coast round Britain.

FALMOUTH – A KEY PORT

Falmouth is one place where I may consider moving the goalposts of my cruising ambitions. Too many cruises are ruined by a pig-headed refusal to modify a declared aim. Sailing is for pleasure and a cruise should be fun. Carrying on regardless is for comic book heroes. I once spent ten days stuck in Harwich waiting for the weather that would take me to the West Country before I came to my senses and had a splendid cruise along the Dutch and Belgium coasts.

FALMOUTH TO LA CORUÑA

As the seagull flies, it is 420 miles from Lizard Point to La Coruña in the north-west corner of Spain; once round Ushant, whatever happens, you are committed to taking it on the chin. Fine, settled weather is an advantage but a week is longer in weather forecasting than in politics. Nowadays it is possible to go to the public library in the centre of Falmouth, and surf the net until you find a suitable forecast. Synoptic charts can be culled from newspapers and the airwaves scoured for shipping forecasts.

KEY PORTS

Many of the boats that start out on an Atlantic Circuit come to a dead stop along the way perhaps because, when taken as a whole, crossing the Atlantic is an intimidating project. In my planning phase some ports stood out as the starting point for a longer than normal passage and at each of these I could choose my next destination from a range of options. I called these ports Key Ports and used them to:

- Delay making a final decision about crossing the Atlantic for as long as possible. A decision to continue held good only to the next port.
- Break the Circuit into manageable chunks and not allow my imagination to be overwhelmed by the distances involved.

You might find it useful to draw up your own Key Port list. Here is mine.

KEY PORT	NEXT PORT	OPTIONS
Falmouth	La Coruña	1 La Coruña via Brittany 2 Mediterranean via French Canals 3 Azores and to the Caribbean 4 Madeira and to the Canaries 5 West coast circumnavigation of UK 6 Go home
La Coruña	Lisbon	1 Iberian cruise 2 Falmouth direct 3 Falmouth via Brittany 4 Azores and to the Caribbean 5 Madeira and to the Canaries
Viano do Castelo/ Lagos	Porto Santo (Madeira)	1 Gibraltar and the Mediterranean 2 Canaries direct 3 Use as cruising base for a season
Madeira	Canaries	1 North Africa and the Mediterranean 2 Gibraltar and the Mediterranean 3 Azores and home
Canaries	Caribbean	1 Iberia direct 2 Gibraltar and Mediterranean 3 Azores and home 4 Use as cruising base for a season

If I sailed west from the Canaries then I reckoned that I was committed to reaching the Caribbean but by then I had made three fairly lengthy passages and was in a far better position to make an informed decision. If I was wrong then I would have to live with my mistake.

In the great days of sail, square-riggers crossing the Bay sailed west until La Coruña bore south and then altered course to keep the Pole Star on their backstays. This simplified their navigation, reduced the chances of being embayed and allowed them to pick up a favourable current worth around ten miles a day. Wise guys on those square-riggers, but I knew better. Don't we all?

ROUTE PLANNING: THE DAILY RUN

How long you expect to be on passage determines the amount of food and water carried and this depends on the route you choose and your expected daily mileage. Once at sea the wind will impose its reality and extra supplies must be carried to allow for over-optimism about your boat's performance.

Your daily mileage depends not only on the winds encountered but on how you sail your boat. A racing boat will chase the slightest wind shift, change sails at the slightest puff and trim sails all day long. A cruising boat will set the sails up and leave them alone until they are crying out for attention. Unless there is a good reason to drive the crew beyond exhaustion there is rarely the manpower or motivation to do the work. I opted for idleness when estimating my daily mileage. You may not.

Ocean route planning thinks big and keeps it simple. Once you have agreed your estimated daily mileage sit down with a routeing chart and dry-sail using the wind roses to give the expected winds along your route. This helps you estimate your time en route. The rhumb line distance from Falmouth to La Coruña is 420 miles but a dog leg to the west brings it up to around 500 miles.

Falmouth to La Coruña

	Estimated daily run	Actual daily run	Actual winds
Day 1	64	99	NW 3/4
Day 2	64	88.5	SW 3/4
Day 3	72	87.5	SW 6/7
Day 4	72	74.6	SW 6/7
Day 5	79	74.6	V 1/2
Day 6	79	77.8	V 1/2
Day 7	79	0	
Totals	509	502	

You may prefer basing your daily mileage on that of similar vessels that have crossed the Atlantic. Looking at almost 150 small boat crossings of the Atlantic from 1886 to the 1960s I found that regardless of the improvements in design and equipment over this period and whether or not they were sailing east to west or west to east, their average speed for the whole trip worked out at half their maximum hull speed. (Maximum hull speed = $1.4 \sqrt{LWL}$ knots.) After 1960, racing yachts dominate the readily accessible published data and skew the figures.

Half *Mintaka's* maximum hull speed is around three knots, a daily run of 72 miles. On this basis, 500 miles would take me almost exactly seven days, which agreed with my wind rose calculations.

Dolphins are a familiar sight on an Atlantic crossing; they love to accompany boats, often enjoying riding the bow wave as you sail along.

HEAVY WEATHER

Noon to noon on my first day out of Falmouth we ran a touch under 100 miles for the first 24 hours and all of it had been under sail. I had not touched the helm or a sheet. The weather forces were displeased. With little change in strength they swung the wind round to the south-west. I hardened sheets and gave up westing. As I put the position on the chart I noticed that we had left the continental shelf behind and were off soundings. This had to mean something.

It did. This was the big boys' league where the wind played hardball. It increased until it was blowing a steady force 6 to 7. Free from the influence of land, this is where Admiral Francis Beaufort's figures on wave heights take on their true meaning and it was not happy reading. Later, in the Trades, calculating wave height, speed and length was a way of passing the time rather than a means of adding to my worries.

I wondered about heaving-to or even lying a-hull but there seemed to be no reason for such drastic measures. *Mintaka* was sailing up the waves at 10°–15° to the general wave front and swooping down their backs before rising to meet the next wave, and she enjoyed it.

WATCH KEEPING

Rest periods were subject to the tyranny of the egg timer. Every 20 minutes it would ring and I would crawl to the hatch, open it and take a look around. If the horizon was empty I would then reset the timer for another 20 minutes.

After three days I was exhausted and tired of the unending discomfort and damp. Some argue that 20 minutes is too long to stay below. It is certainly too short to rest. The inevitable happened: I fell asleep and woke up six hours later. What had I done? I scanned the horizon in panic. It was empty and *Mintaka* was quite unconcerned. I relaxed. There was no way I could cross an ocean on 20 minute catnaps. The egg timer would have to go.

WATCH-AND-WATCH

When I crossed the Bay in *Margo*, a friend came as crew and we worked watch-and-watch with dog-watches so that each day the watches moved round. This is a good system, with plenty of scope to catch up on rest once we fell into its rhythm. Some vary this system by working four-hour watches during the day and three hours at night, though by the time the watch is handed over this system cuts bunk time to just over two hours which is not enough for a decent rest. Short watches make sense only in heavy weather when those in the cockpit suffer. In his book *The Last Grain Race*, Eric Newby describes a watch-and-watch system using a mixture of four-, five-, and six-hour watches. It has much to recommend it.

MOTHER WATCH

If there are three aboard, a mother watch system works well. Each day one person is taken off watch and is responsible for all cooking and the ship's housework but is (almost) guaranteed an unbroken night's sleep while the other two work watch-and-watch. The small print on the guarantee says the 'mother' is on standby and will be the first to be called out if an extra hand is needed.

If there are four in the crew, a straightforward watch system gives 12 unbroken hours off watch every day, but like any straight rota system, opens up the debate on who should be on standby. The mother watch system provides one answer. Keeping dog-watches means that everyone has their fair share of nasty night hours.

If, like me, you begin by believing that a watch system that had served well on coastal and offshore passages will work for longer ocean passages then you may ask too much of your crew. Be prepared to rethink. Almost any watch system can be made to work; a good system is one which sails the boat efficiently, plays to people's strengths, shares the workload fairly, minimises time on watch, maximises time off watch and has the willing support of the crew.

WATCH KEEPING SYSTEMS

CREW OF TWO

Watch-and-watch

Time	On Watch Day 1	On Watch Day 2
0000 – 0400	Tom	Dick
0400 – 0800	Dick	Tom
0800 – 1200	Tom	Dick
1200 – 1600	Dick	Tom
1600 – 1800	Tom	Dick
1800 – 2000	Dick	Tom
2000 – 2400	Tom	Dick

Moshulu system

Time	On Watch Day 1	On Watch Day 2
0000 – 0400	Tom	Dick
0400 – 0800	Dick	Tom
0800 – 1300	Tom	Dick
1300 – 1900	Dick	Tom
1900 – 2400	Tom	Dick

CREW OF THREE

Four hours on, eight hours off

Time	On Watch Day 1	On Watch Day 2	On Watch Day 3
0000 – 0400	Tom	Dick	Harry
0400 – 0800	Dick	Harry	Tom
0800 – 1200	Harry	Tom	Dick
1200 – 1600	Tom	Dick	Harry
1600 – 1800	Dick	Harry	Tom
1800 – 2000	Harry	Tom	Dick
2000 – 2400	Tom	Dick	Harry

This system requires that either the person just gone off watch or the person next on watch is nominated as standby to assist with any manoeuvres.

Mother watch system

Time	On Watch Day 1	On Watch Day 2	On Watch Day 3
0000 – 0400	Tom	Harry	Dick
0400 – 0800	Dick	Tom	Harry
0800 – 1200	Tom	Harry	Dick
1200 – 1600	Dick	Tom	Harry
1600 – 1800	Tom	Harry	Dick
1800 – 2000	Dick	Tom	Harry
2000 – 2400	Tom	Harry	Dick
'Mother'	Harry	Dick	Tom

In this system 'mother' is always on standby and called out to assist with any manoeuvres.

CREW OF FOUR

Four hours on: eight hours off

Time	On Watch Day 1	On Watch Day 2	On Watch Day 3	On Watch Day 4
0000 – 0400	Tom	Bill	Harry	Dick
0400 – 0800	Dick	Tom	Bill	Harry
0800 – 1200	Harry	Dick	Tom	Bill
1200 – 1600	Bill	Harry	Dick	Tom
1600 – 1800	Tom	Bill	Harry	Dick
1800 – 2000	Dick	Tom	Bill	Harry
2000 – 2400	Harry	Dick	Tom	Bill

This system requires that someone off watch is nominated as standby to assist with any manoeuvres.

HEAVY WEATHER LESSONS

Nothing lasts forever, even heavy weather. By mid-morning on the third day the wind had moderated. But the gale had been useful. Apart from revising my watch keeping system I had discovered that *Mintaka* could sail upwind over the long ocean rollers and with the correct sail plan Alfred the Navik was happy to play his part in steering. In my home waters, going upwind under sail in heavy weather is out of the question. In the North Sea's short, steep seas, *Mintaka*, and later *Margo*, may appear to have sheeted hard and be sailing close-hauled but the reality is slow, sideways progress as we slam, dunk and stop at every other wave.

In these conditions I choose between heaving-to, lying a-hull, motor-sailing upwind or running away. I expected similar but worse off soundings but had forgotten that though ocean waves may be big and steep they are also long with a typical period of six to eight seconds. It is the difference between trying, and failing, to climb a cliff face and plodding up a long hillside. It was not pleasant. Heavy weather is never enjoyable but it was far more comfortable than I expected.

I had stumbled upon what became my standard deep-sea, heavy weather technique and it worked even though the wind blew so hard that *Mintaka* (and later *Margo*) was under bare poles. I called it my cork mode.

Masts do break at sea; be prepared for a fairly long wait in harbour for a replacement.

For really horrible conditions I carried a parachute sea anchor but never found the opportunity to use it. As a first-time bonus I discovered that noon-to-noon we had made good just over 80 miles but it had cost all and more of the westing I had built up. We were well into the Bay and east of La Coruña.

It would be wrong to over-emphasise bad weather. Everyone meets it and no one enjoys it but passages on the Atlantic Circuit are made at times to avoid bad weather and although when it happens it seems to last forever, it makes up a very small proportion of your sea time.

OCEAN NAVIGATION

There were nearly 180 miles remaining and every one of them was spent discussing, with a fitful and petulant wind, how best to travel south-west. Apart from a couple of hours late one evening, the sky remained overcast and the sextant remained in its box. Crossing the Bay many years ago, I had my baptism of using a sextant without some other means of confirming our position. Two or three times a day I would appear on deck and go through the ritual of shooting the sun or a selection of stars before retiring to the chart table to do my arithmetic. It bruised my confidence when I discovered that the crew were betting on how far I would miss La Coruña and when land did appear, some claimed to be unsure whether we were looking at France, Spain or Portugal. A few still claim they were right.

Not that long ago, attempting to cross an ocean without being competent at celestial navigation would have been criticised as foolhardy and while it may not be a black art, there is as much skill in using the tables that accompany the arithmetic as there is in understanding what you are doing. On small boats, and sometimes not so small boats, pin-point accuracy is rare and, at best, a fix is only possible two or three times a day: between times, positions are obtained from DR calculations.

Columbus relied exclusively on DR for his first crossing. His first attempt at finding his latitude by celestial navigation was made at anchor off Cuba. He used a quadrant, had an error of 20°, which put him close to Cape Cod. His subsequent efforts were no better and to the end Columbus remained a confirmed DR navigator.

He would have loved GPS. It has changed navigation from an art to a form of computer literacy. No knowledge or understanding is required beyond the ability to press keys and follow the on-screen commands. On ocean passages waypoints may be days or weeks apart. Variety comes from weather routeing and navigation demands little more than noting the noon position and the daily work.

THE DAILY WORK

This is a hangover from my pre-GPS days and describes calculating your DR position using the courses and distances steered from one noon to the next. It is helpful when the scale of the chart makes accurate plotting difficult. Columbus would have been familiar with the daily work. He would have used toleta, or traverse board, to resolve course and distance into differences of latitude and longitude. Later traverse tables were used to provide the answer but a cheap scientific calculator is easier and quicker. By comparing your DR position with that given by the GPS it is possible to make a fairly accurate estimate of the effect of the current and leeway.

Ocean currents give the illusion that they follow the arrows on pilot charts. Not so. Currents are more complex. Pilot charts and textbook illustrations deal in generalities masking meanders, eddies and swirls that go where, how and when they please.

Off soundings in the northern hemisphere surface water is reckoned to move at 45° or less to the right of the wind at 1–2% of the average wind speed over the previous two or three days. In soundings the direction may be as little as 15° to the right of the wind. Never assume that currents play by the rules. You may think that a favourable current is sweeping you along, but the daily work may show that it is taking you backwards or shoving you sideways.

ARRIVAL IN LA CORUÑA

La Coruña is an important key port. Arrival there gives the opportunity to review your first long passage and ask if you wish to continue. If not, then you can sail back, perhaps via Brittany, or go down the Iberian coast into the Mediterranean and home through the French canals. This is really a holding decision, for you can change your mind and carry on for the Caribbean before reaching the Mediterranean.

In the marina I saw familiar yachts from Falmouth but there were many strangers. There were boats that had crept along the north coast of France to explore Brittany and the north coast of Spain; others had crossed the North Sea from Scandinavia, passed through the Caledonian Canal, and joined up with yachts from the west coast of Scotland to cruise the Irish coast before heading south.

GALACIAN INTERLUDE

It is a well-kept secret that blue-water cruisers are reluctant sailors taking their barnacle-encrusted craft to sea only when every other option is not just closed but bolted, barred and barricaded against them. As my copy of *The Sober Sailor's Sensible Bedside Handbook* puts it, 'A properly planned trans-Atlantic cruise is a series of day sails to make new friends and discover new cruising grounds separated by the occasional and unavoidable longer passage.' I looked at Galacia, the north-west coast of Spain, through new eyes and as a place to linger and explore, not pass through.

This is part of Europe's Celtic fringe, a fascinating and largely unspoilt cruising ground, a region proud of its seafaring traditions and eager to welcome visitors; an ideal place to spend the dog days of summer. The coastline is saw-toothed by flooded river valleys called rias, each one an easy day-sail from its neighbours and all welcome visitors. July and August is the fiesta season. Every Spanish city, town, hamlet and crossroads has its patron saint and every saint's birthday is an excuse for a holiday and a grand celebration announced days beforehand by fusillades of fireworks that sound like the Spanish army rehearsing. On weekdays you can find the nearest fiesta by using the lazy Portuguese trade winds to propel you towards the sounds of battle and the nearest tapas bar. Saturday and Sunday bring fireworks galore, dancing and lots of music. Each fiesta must take months of preparation but even in a city like Vigo there is a sense of great spontaneity, of everyone doing their own thing and having a good time. Progress south slows to a cheerful crawl, fuelled by grilled sardines, churos and red wine.

CRUISING PORTUGAL

The Rio Minho, a few miles south of Bayona, marks the border between Spain and Portugal and a dramatic change in the coastline. The wide mouthed rias with their creeks and inlets are replaced by an undulating cliffy shore broken by rivers entering the sea over shallow bars. When heavy onshore weather displaces the Portuguese Trades, this coast is a fearsome place. Entering or leaving harbour is impossible. If at sea you stay out, and if in harbour you retire to the nearest café and thank your lucky stars. In 1995 I was trapped for days in Lisbon and in 1999 in Viano do Castelo, where I was stuck for almost a fortnight; I spent my time celebrating its fiesta. It attracts visitors from all over Portugal with some of the loudest bands I have heard.

Somewhere between Viano do Castelo and Lagos on the Algarve it is time to find another key port and make a final decision whether to continue towards Porto Santo and Madeira or make for the Mediterranean. Returning north is not a sensible option unless you are prepared to motor into the teeth of the Portuguese Trades and the current. A third option is to leave your boat in one of the many marinas and use that as a base for a season or two. The journey home has not yet become horribly expensive.

TO THE MADEIRAS

Undecided where to go, I sailed from Lisbon at the first hint of the weather moderating. In my haste I got the tides wrong and paid penance. *Mintaka* shuffled down the Tagus like an old woman and I hid under my embarrassment. The wind was dropping but the seas were still running high as we took the main channel to the open sea instead of the inshore shortcut. A cruise liner overtook us and it was comforting to see that their martinis were shaken rather than stirred.

Those seas made up my mind. It seemed unlikely they would moderate much in the next 24 hours and, in their present state, approaching any harbour on this coast would be an unnecessary excitement. *Mintaka* agreed so we unrolled some jib and pointed the bows towards Porto Santo.

Once clear of the coast it was a glorious sail in an empty sea under a star-filled sky. Porto Santo, 26 miles from Madeira, is only 10 miles long and 4 miles wide, a small target in a big ocean. I believed the GPS but it was comforting when after 6 days mountain peaks and every yacht heading for the Caribbean popped over the horizon.

The island's only harbour, Porto do Porto Santo, is on the south coast, and yachts sailing

Fig 9 *Passage between Lisbon and Porto Santo.*

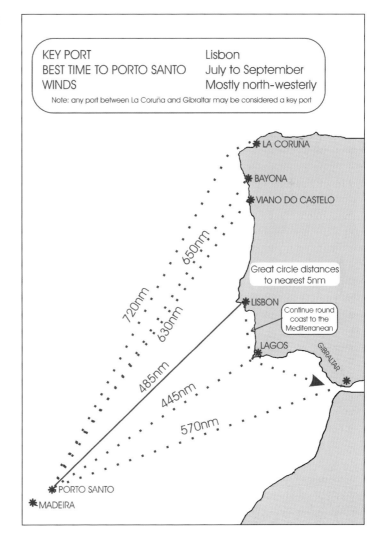

from the Mediterranean, Spain, Portugal and Northern Europe all aim for the south-west corner of the island before racing for the finish line at the harbour. It is like Piccadilly Circus and where the Atlantic Circuit really begins. From now on every yacht you meet intends to cross the Atlantic, and most are blue-water virgins, pleased to have come so far but uncertain of what lies ahead.

In 1996 there was the choice of anchoring outside or inside the harbour, with a remote possibility of a berth in the small marina, but by 1999 life had moved on. Moorings have been laid inside the harbour, a travel hoist has appeared, and a boatyard is growing. There is a dive school, scooter hire and there is talk of opening a casino. A new, bigger supermarket has opened, making provisioning for the passage to the Canaries much easier.

PORTO SANTO

Porto Santo has a beautiful beach and burying yourself in the sand to take advantage of its medicinal properties is popular with holiday makers from Madeira. Back in the 15th century, Columbus married the daughter of the governor of Porto Santo and in 1995 his house, the beach and some windmills were the island's only tourist attractions. The rest of the island could star in a spaghetti western.

I did not expect to stay long. Several weeks later I found the energy to move on to Madeira. This is the Porto Santo effect where mañana is a term of indecent haste. When Joao Goncalves Zarco and Tristao Vaz Teixeira became the first Europeans to land on Porto Santo in 1419 it took them a year to sail 26 miles and 'discover' Madeira.

The big adventure starts: leaving Las Palmas bound for the Caribbean.

MADEIRA

Although Madeira was uninhabited when Zarco eventually arrived, it is reckoned that the Phoenicians reached it first and an Italian map dated 1351 shows both islands. If you wish to explore Madeira but believe Funchal's marina will be too busy (it is) and are reluctant to test the poor holding of the outside anchorage (it is awful), there is a daily ferry and regular flights from Porto Santo. Once it was necessary to visit Madeira to obtain a permit to stop at the Salvage Islands on the way to the Canaries but now that can be arranged from Porto Santo.

It would be a pity to miss Madeira. Funchal has grown by spreading up the hillside and when you reach the top of the town it is traditional to slide back down in a wicker sledge. For the energetic there is *levada* walking. *Levadas* are irrigation channels cut into the hillside to bring water from the wet north of the island to the dry south. Slaves began digging them in the 16th century, often hanging over cliffs in baskets to carve out the channel. Now they stretch for over a thousand kilometres and walking the paths alongside is a popular and occasionally spectacular pastime. If you go hiking along the *levadas* wear boots and take waterproofs and warm clothing.

Apart from Porto Santo, the Madeiras include the Ilhas Desertas and the Ilhas Selvagems. Both are nature reserves and the Desertas are home to monk seals, which are one of the ten most threatened species on the list of animals near extinction.

LIFE AT ANCHOR

The further you sail the more your attitude towards anchoring changes. Marinas provide the convenience of life ashore while creating the illusion of being afloat. They make folk lazy. As night falls the sails come down, engines fire up and bows rise out of the water as everyone makes for the nearest pontoon. Anchoring is for picnics or waiting for the tide. By this stage of the Atlantic Circuit anchoring is preferred to marinas and by the time you reach the Caribbean most boats anchor for most of the time.

Fig 10 *Using two anchors.*

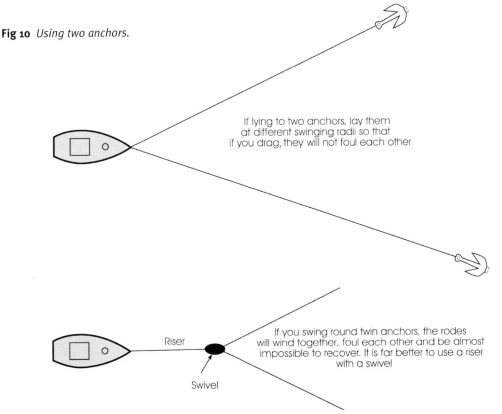

If lying to two anchors, lay them at different swinging radii so that if you drag, they will not foul each other

Riser

Swivel

If you swing round twin anchors, the rodes will wind together, foul each other and be almost impossible to recover. It is far better to use a riser with a swivel

Entire communities swing at anchor. Yachts are left unattended when crews go ashore to shop, play tourist or party. Come bedtime, folk take to their bunks until breakfast. Anchor watches are unknown. The confidence to do this comes partly from lying to a steady wind but mostly from lots of chain and a bower anchor at least one size above that recommended for your yacht.

Many yachts carry a second, equally large anchor of a different type ready to be let go. Second anchors often live on the pushpit as stern anchors are useful to reduce swing in busy anchorages, or if you are lying to the swell in a cross wind, an anchor laid to an angle to the stern is used to haul the yacht round until its bows are pointing into the seas. This is much more comfortable. In really busy anchorages, textbooks suggest using a Bahamian moor but I have never seen this for real, even in the Bahamas.

TYPE OF ANCHOR

Although some swear by one particular type of anchor and have the figures to prove it, in my experience the best anchor is a tractor engine, encapsulated in concrete and buried deep. Failing that, big is beautiful and it helps to have at least two different anchors to meet differing conditions. Many yachts carry a third very large 'thank God' anchor just in case.

THE WEAKEST LINK

An anchor system is only as safe as its weakest link. If you choose an oversized anchor then chain, shackles, swivels, bitts, anchor roller and winch must be sized to match and the work to make this possible is best done during the refit before you sail, for it demands major engineering.

Whether you use chain, chain and warp or

An idyllic, peaceful mooring in the Saintes.

all warp depends on you. Boats appear to sheer less with all chain but yachts on warp do not snatch quite as much, and those using all chain often have a snubbing line tied to their anchor chain. Warp is lighter to haul in than chain but it does not self stow and it is liable to chafe where it lies along the bottom or wraps round a coral head. Perhaps these are arguments in favour of a mixture of chain and warp. Warp is also likely to chafe where it enters the boat but this is prevented by using long lengths of thick plastic hose.

CHECKING THE ANCHOR

Most anchoring takes place in depths of between five and ten metres. If you desire

peace of mind, and space permits, then forget the rule that says three times the depth for chain and five times for warp and let it all hang out. You bought it to use when anchoring, not as ballast, so why not use it? Once you reach warmer waters, it is no hardship to dive, visually check how the anchor is set and, if necessary, pick it up and move it around until you are happy. A mask and fins are enough for this task.

The use of a 'kellet', 'chum' or 'angel' to improve the catenary and holding power of an anchor is well known but few boats carry one just in case. If needed, one can be easily made up from a short length of chain and almost any small weight such as dive weights or grapnel type anchor.

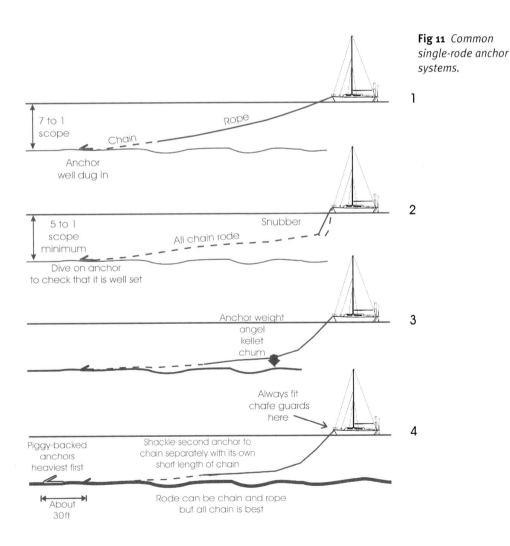

Fig 11 *Common single-rode anchor systems.*

1

7 to 1 scope

Rope

Chain

Anchor well dug In

2

5 to 1 scope minimum

Snubber

All chain rode

Dive on anchor to check that it is well set

3

Anchor weight angel kellet chum

4

Always fit chafe guards here

Piggy-backed anchors heaviest first

Shackle second anchor to chain separately with its own short length of chain

About 30 ft

Rode can be chain and rope but all chain is best

ENTERING AN ANCHORAGE

I admire those who have the confidence to roar into a busy anchorage, throw the anchor over the side, leap into the dinghy and be ashore before the anchor has reached the bottom. For me, it is a fraught time. Picking the right spot is not easy and I live in terror of fouling someone's anchor or dropping back onto another yacht. I creep in slowly and when I find a vacant parking place I first check that its emptiness is not because it hides a sandbank, wreck or reef. If there is life on nearby yachts I casually enquire about the holding and where their anchors lie. Evaluating their replies needs careful judgement for some yachts seeking solitude will tell fibs. If I am happy that all is well I go close to the stern of the yacht that will end up immediately ahead of me, lower the anchor and drop back into my chosen spot. When I stop, the engine can be run astern for a couple of moments to make sure the anchor is dug in.

GOING ASHORE

Life at anchor means running a shuttle service between the boat and the shore and a good dinghy is essential as a ferry and a bulk carrier. Sometimes there is a dinghy dock and a dinghy anchor thrown over the stern as a kedge prevents damage by holding the dinghy off the dock while ashore. More often it is a beach landing through surf, with the threat of capsize for added interest. If an inversion is likely then take papers, cameras, cash and valuables ashore in a waterproof bag. At night, dinghies do not always show lights but carrying a torch is prudent, and if you wish to find your own yacht easily a good anchor light helps guide you home. If you are worried about draining your batteries it is simple to rig a light-sensitive switch that will switch the anchor light on as darkness falls.

A small outboard engine takes the strain out of rowing. Otherwise it is important to choose a dinghy that rows well into a head wind. Except for short distances, soft bottomed inflatables are tiring to row. A small RIB is a good workhorse but is at its best with an outboard. Hard dinghies are the most versatile but are heavy and difficult to stow. Inflating and deflating dinghies is a chore so they spend a lot of their time in the water gathering their fair share of weed. They do not take kindly to scraping tools, and cleaning their hulls before weed builds up is a regular task. Patches and adhesive should be carried for small repairs. If you are competent at this type of work then a spare valve or two might be useful.

TOWING THE DINGHY

The only way to discover how your dinghy tows is to take it to sea behind you. It is an education to watch it surf down a wave as though it is about to vault over the stern and then, when collision seems inevitable, it skids to a stop and waits for the tow line to jerk it into motion like a recalcitrant mule. This strains the dinghy fittings beyond their design limits time after time, mile after mile. Sometimes dinghies fill with water and sometimes in strong winds inflatables take to the air and always crash land upside down. It is a good idea to take everything out of the dinghy before setting off. Sometimes they fill with water and act as a drogue. Bailing a dinghy at sea is never simple and can be dangerous. Anyone bailing the dinghy at sea should wear a lifejacket and be attached to the mother ship.

There are supporters of long tows and short tows; of single and multiple attachment points for the tow line on the dinghy and at the stern of your yacht. Most systems work some of the time in some conditions. As a precaution against fouling the prop, try fitting the sort of floats used to mark swimming pool lanes along the tow line. Towing a dinghy is never straightforward and the only certainty about your choice of dinghy is that your views when you start out will not be the same when you return home.

DOG ISLANDS CRUISE

After leaving Porto Santo or Madeira, if the weather is settled, spend a few days visiting the Salvage Islands. This is a scattering of islands and associated, and often uncharted, rocks and shoals arranged in two groups about ten miles apart. They lie, more or less, on the route between Madeira and the Canaries, waiting for a visit from the careless navigator, hence their name. They are now a nature reserve and uninhabited apart from a couple of wardens based on Selvagem Grande who will be delighted to see you and show you around their small world.

There are three official anchorages, two on Selvagem Grande and one on Selvagem Pequena that must be used, but they are not particularly good in unsettled weather.

There are lights on both Selvagem Grande and Selvagem Pequena but do not be surprised if either or both are not working.

After the Salvage Islands it is usual to aim for the east end of the Canaries. Graciosa at the east end of the chain is good landfall and from there cruise slowly westwards through the archipelago arriving on Gran Canaria, Tenerife or La Gomera by late October or early November.

The nine Canary Islands are volcanic and still have active volcanoes with around 20 major eruptions spread throughout the chain since 1341. The original islanders were the fair skinned, blue eyed, blond-haired Guanche. Later the Arabs set up trading centres on the islands and they were followed by the Genoese, French and Spanish whose claims to the islands in the early 15th century were finally recognised in 1469. The King of Mauritania was impressed by the fierce dogs (*canis* in Latin) found in the islands and so the islands were called the Canaries, but Pliny was right when he called them the 'fortunate isles'.

Little is known about the Guanche and there has been some fanciful speculation on their origins. Recently the remains of step pyramids similar to those found in Mexico, Peru and Mesopotamia were found on Tenerife and they provide food for thought about pre-Columbian links between the new and the old worlds. Did the Guanche, like us, gather each November in the Muelle Deportivo on Las Palmas to make ready for their transatlantic voyage?

6 Final Preparations at Las Palmas

I left home believing that each time I reached port, crowds would gather to greet the intrepid transatlantic sailor. Nothing is further from the truth. When you arrive in port you fight to find a berth, not your way through the welcoming crowds. In late autumn, the Muelle Deportivo at Las Palmas on Gran Canaria is crowded with vessels from Europe and the Mediterranean.

This is where your Atlantic crossing starts. The air is heavy with views and news on blue-water passage making, for amongst its other characteristics the Muelle Deportivo is a rumour factory where whispers, especially horror stories, are quickly passed from boat to boat. The real surprise is not the number of boats crossing the Atlantic but that any sail at all.

To make the most of the Caribbean season the charter fleet begins leaving in mid-November. Berths inside the marina are at a premium and the anchorage outside is crowded. Even with the unfinished marina extensions pressed into service it was just the same in 1998. The marinas on the island's south coast are fully booked months in advance.

RALLIES

In 1995 some two hundred boats left with the ARC at the end of November. Ocean rallies are growing in popularity. The ARC, grand daddy of them all, was started by Jimmy Cornell in 1986 and sails each year from Las Palmas to Rodney Bay in St Lucia. Rallies are big business and very welcome at any port they visit but the number of boats involved can also temporarily stretch port facilities and amenities beyond breaking point.

Some boats taking part in rallies believe that when they arrive at an official rally port of call they have first claim on what facilities are available. To them, anyone not in the rally is sailing on the cheap and 'independent' becomes a term of abuse. On the other hand 'independents' regard themselves as the true guardians of the blue-water cruising traditions. In 1995 there was even an association for non-ARC boats, the NARC. Membership was optional and free. It had its own flag, a yellow square defaced by the symbol of your choice, and its only rule was that you made your own rules as you went along. The truth is that there is much to be said on both sides and enough sea for everyone.

RATIONING AND FOOD

I like eating, but being ignorant of proteins, vitamins and a lousy cook, provisioning is a task I love to delegate. This is hard when you are sailing single-handed. There is no simple answer on how much food is enough. I have fallen into the habit of rationing for the maximum expected time on passage plus half as much again. For an Atlantic crossing this means carrying food for 50 days with fresh fruit and vegetables appearing on menus daily for the first month. This may seem over the top but it is all eaten eventually.

Boats of all types, shapes and sizes can be seen assembling at Las Palmas for the Atlantic hike.
Top left: Loose Moose 2, an unusual Phil Bolger design seen at Las Palmas.
Top right: A home-built 6m Swedish yacht preparing to make the crossing.
Bottom: An 8m double-ender lies among the big boats.

DAILY MENU

I have tried writing daily menus for a week and buying food to match menus for six weeks. The result is chaos because this demands an orderly stowage system, good record keeping and disciplined eating habits. There are days when the urge to eat or cook has vanished and other days where the only way to pass the time is to eat.

I plan to have muesli or porridge with coffee for breakfast, a snack lunch and decent evening meal with a selection of sweet and savoury nibbles to fill any gaps. Rather than shop for particular menus I make sure that I have on board enough food for 50 breakfasts, 50 snacks and 50 main meals and bagfuls of nibbles. It sounds haphazard but it works.

KEEPING FOOD FRESH

On the way to the Canaries I experimented with how long fresh food, especially fruit and vegetables, remained edible and was pleasantly surprised. Lesson one was to avoid supermarket vegetables. They chill their fruit and vegetables and chilled produce does not keep for long. It is far better to seek out the farmers' markets and buy local produce. It may not look so pretty, and may come in odd sizes and shapes but it is fresh, keeps longer and tastes better.

The second lesson was to take nothing aboard until it had been washed in a mild bleach solution of about a tablespoon of chlorine bleach to a bucket of water. This kills bugs and avoids the danger of giving members of the insect kingdom a free ride to the sun.

Hard vegetables such as potatoes, onions and carrots last quite a long time. Apples and oranges keep fairly well and limes and lemons can be squeezed to make lemonade-style drinks. Green bananas last well but they ripen en masse and create a glut, although I am told that when ripe they can be peeled and dried in the sun, making tasty snacks.

Fruit and vegetables keep badly if wrapped in polythene bags or sealed in plastic containers. Firm fruits and vegetables prefer being hung in nets along the deckhead; store soft varieties in open, mesh plastic boxes such as milk crates. Check all fruit and vegetables daily and throw out any that are going bad. It is said that pineapples kept with other fruit will cause them to go bad.

It is also said that eggs go off when the yolk is allowed to rest upon the shell and the best way to extend their life is to turn them upside down every other day. Some people swear by coating the porous egg shells in petroleum jelly to keep bacteria at bay. Nuts, and dried fruit like raisins, figs, prunes and apricots, keep well and provide useful, nourishing snacks. Cheese sweats but lasts reasonably well; any mould can be cut off to reveal the good cheese underneath. Canned butter is available in some stores but margarine in plastic tubs keeps well even though it may melt during the day.

Bacon and fresh meat never last more than a couple of days but dried meats, such as salami and Spanish Cerrano ham, last for weeks.

Unsliced fresh white or wholemeal bread keeps longer than sliced. Rye bread remains edible for ages and Spanish supermarkets sell packets of toast, which last for a couple of weeks. If you have an oven, then baking bread is not difficult and it can also be cooked in a pressure cooker. It is also possible to prepare good bread substitutes in a frying pan. White flour keeps well but wholemeal flour goes off after a couple of months.

Milk is no problem. Long life UHT milk is almost indistinguishable from fresh milk and there are excellent dried whole milk powders that come close to tasting like milk, but you have to be in the Canaries before this type is in the shops. Canned evaporated milk is palatable but condensed milk is only for those with a sweet tooth.

With fresh fruit and vegetables for a month and milk all the way across, the risk of scurvy or vitamin deficiencies should be minimal, but without a fridge or freezer the remainder of my food supplies was made up of rice (brown when I could find it), pasta and canned or dried food.

The Canaries are the last chance to stock up on fresh produce before the crossing.

BREAD SUBSTITUTES

On passage it is easy to become obsessed with the need for fresh bread especially if you do not have an oven.

PAN BREAD

I was given this recipe when at anchor in the Saintes and it works well. It is a soda bread but cooked in a frying pan instead of being baked. It has the great advantage of being quick to make and economical in gas.

- Four heaped tablespoons strong flour
- 1 heaped teaspoon of baking powder
- Salt to taste
- Water

Mix everything together to make a soft dough and roll it out until it is about half an inch thick. Heat a little oil in a heavy frying pan and fry the dough for about ten minutes with a lid on the frying pan. It should rise a bit and set on the bottom. Turn it over, fry for another five minutes and eat it the same day as it does not keep well.

For variety use half wholemeal flour or substitute oats or bran for some of the flour or add grated onion or cheese or use sugar instead of salt, throw in some dried fruit and call it cake.

POTATO SCONES

My Grandmother used to make these and they go well with fried eggs and tomatoes, canned or fresh.

- Potatoes (dried potato will do)
- Flour
- Salt to taste
- A small knob of margarine

Mash or sieve the potatoes. Add the salt and margarine. Knead in the flour. The ratio of flour to potato is about 1 to 4 (ie one ounce of flour for every four ounces of potato). Roll out and cut into rounds with a cup. Fry in a hot heavy frying pan for two to three minutes. Turn over and fry for another two to three minutes. If any are left over they can be fried with bacon and eggs for tomorrow's breakfast.

DRIED FOOD

Dried peas and beans (there is a huge variety of dried beans) need soaking overnight before cooking. They are best cooked in a pressure cooker and go well with rice, or fish or both. Along with lentils, onions, tomatoes (canned or fresh) and rice, they can form the basis of a decent meal besides being good sources of protein, carbohydrates, fibre and vitamin B. Some people extol the virtues of soya that comes in granule form pretending to be ground meat or stew-sized chunks. I have tried both the basic soya protein and the proprietary ready flavoured types and liked neither but if it is to your taste it is a useful addition to the larder. Although I suspect that they are low in vitamins, canned meat, fruit and vegetables are useful standbys.

Dried vegetables, rice, flour and pasta, even if bought in sealed polythene packets, can harbour weevils. Keep packets separate. I used Ziploc bags and put them inside Tupperware-type boxes that also protected against damp. When a packet was opened it was emptied into its container – glass jars with rubber sealed lids are good – and carefully checked. Dried vegetables, rice and pasta should be rinsed before use. Sieving flour or sugar is supposed to be one way of removing weevils but on the couple of occasions I found them the entire packet went overboard.

Variety is provided by spices. Curry powder is the obvious standby but depending on your palate, and expertise, other spices can make the same ingredients taste like Chinese or Italian cooking, or in my case, just different. It is amazing how many ways corned beef can be disguised.

CANNED FOOD

Canned food can be expensive in the Caribbean so stock up in the Canaries. If you come across cheap supplies that keep, then buy as much as you can afford and have space for. Good examples are rum in Venezuela and wine in the Canaries.

It is supposed to be good practice to remove all labels from cans, and identify their contents in paint or felt tip pen before coating them in varnish. The intention is to protect them from rust. I have never taken this precaution and I do not know anyone who has. Instead, I stow cans in large plastic tubs which keeps them dry. If cans get soaked in sea water, rinse in fresh water and leave to dry. Ring-pull cans are vulnerable if they are soaked. This happened to me once and I lost three cans of tuna.

SALTING, DRYING AND BOTTLING FOOD

For those who have the inclination, it is possible to salt, dry or bottle shop-bought food to make it last longer but the skills for this far exceed my culinary expertise.

FRESH WATER SUPPLIES

I was concerned about having sufficient fresh water. I had often read that it was possible to survive comfortably on half a gallon a day. I assumed this was the more generous imperial gallon and on the way south I made several half-hearted attempts at monitoring my daily consumption by filling a two-litre (3.5 pints) plastic bottle and using that as a measure. Provided this water is reserved for drinking, cooking and cleaning your teeth, then half a gallon per day is adequate.

The liquid in canned vegetables, fruit and soft drinks added another couple of pints and gave me a cushion against errors. I also had two solar showers that would give me a weekly fresh water shower and could be added to the drinking water in an emergency. I discovered, the hard way, that sea water is too salty for cooking but I found that by adding a generous dollop of washing up liquid it is fine for cleaning dishes and me.

But would these lessons from temperate waters hold true in the tropics? Would I need more water to survive in the heat? I increased my margin of safety by carrying water for 60 days and planned to top up in every rain shower but never did. It was more than enough and I was never thirsty.

But I would not recommend less than half a gallon per person per day, for this allowance is close to the edge of civilised living. Survival is possible on half as much but for normal passage-making it would require considerable self-discipline and run the risk of discomfort. Boats with bigger tanks and water makers will be more generous but some restraint will be necessary and it may be prudent to switch off pressurised water systems and ration fresh water by pumping up by hand.

MODIFICATIONS

The Canaries are a good place to make those last minute modifications and improvements. With well over a thousand miles under the keel, opinions on what works and what doesn't have firmed up and there are a number of good chandlers and marine outlets in Las Palmas. If they cannot supply what you need then it is easy and not too expensive to have equipment sent out from Europe or the USA or brought out by a new member of crew. Lastly, and most importantly, there is access to a huge reservoir of skills. One of the main differences between a blue-water cruise and a summer holiday afloat is that the Blue-Water Co-operative Inc supplements commercial shoreside facilities.

THE BLUE-WATER CO-OPERATIVE

Circumstances make every blue-water sailor a jack of all trades although only a very few are master of all, but in every anchorage there is a huge, informal pool of skills and on every cruiser is a hoard of hard-to-find odds and ends. Need an electrics specialist, a sailmaker, an engineer, a rigger, or a computer expert?

Carlisle Bay, Barbados: the first Caribbean anchorage for many yachts.

Short of a widget with a left-handed thread? Somewhere amongst the mass of boats is the person with the skills or item you need and it is possible they are looking for someone with your skills. Ideas can be developed and most problems solved over a glass or two at the local bar.

CHARTS

If, like me, you were unsure what charts you would need, this is also a good time to sort out your chart portfolio. Most yachts have on board one or two charts of the Caribbean so if you get them together you can make up a decent Caribbean portfolio. Since DMA charts can be photocopied, a group of sailors putting their charts together and trotting along to the local copy shop benefits everyone.

CREW CHANGES

The Canaries are also a first-rate place for crew members to take a break and go home or to change over. Those with limited time can fly out to join the crossing to the Caribbean or fly home from the Canaries.

FLIGHTS

The Canaries are probably the last chance for an inexpensive flight home and if you can pick up a spare seat on a holiday charter it can be very cheap. The first rule in keeping airfares down is to fly to and from airports with lots of international flights. If there is a significant number of package holiday flights so much the better. Flights to obscure destinations may be romantic but they cost more. Try to avoid internal connecting flights for they are always expensive. Ask around, somebody is bound to have made the same trip recently. Some countries, Guatemala for instance, adds a 20% tax on airline tickets.

Not every travel agent offers the same range of flights, some offer better value than others. Check out various ticket combinations. Sometimes it is cheaper to buy a return ticket even if only flying one way; avoid expensive high season flights, and, if possible, try to avoid a gap of over two months between flying out and returning. Most airlines consider this reason enough to charge more. Booking early can mean a cheap seat but this may restrict changing flights or dates.

7 Radios and Communications

RADIO

Ready to go but unwilling to sail, I was busy with small, unnecessary, tasks in a feeble effort to delay the inevitable, when Bill from *Aloisius* dropped by. 'You don't have an SSB receiver.' It was a statement, not a question. 'Take this.' Brushing aside my protests, he handed over an expensive and suspiciously new-looking portable SSB receiver together with a list of radio schedules.

Bill's loan of a SSB receiver was a kind, generous gesture, typical of pontoon life. The comradeship was akin to a mountain base camp preparing for a summit attempt.

HF RADIOS

Without much thought I had dismissed long-range communications as beyond my reach. HF (or short-wave) transceivers are expensive to buy and greedy on battery power to use and back in 1995 they were the exception, not the rule, on yachts. What I had not considered at all was a cheaper HF receiver, usually called a single sideband (SSB) radio for short. Instead I had bought a very cheap short-wave receiver that would bring in the BBC World Service and other commercial broadcasts but not marine or ham radio transmissions.

DOUBLE SIDEBAND

SSB and HF are often used as synonyms. Properly, the HF band is the part of the radio spectrum equating to the short-wave band and SSB a method of transmitting signals used in that band. For an HF signal to carry a voice or music audio signals then a band of

audio signals is added to the carrier signal. This is called modulation and the oldest system of modulation is called amplitude modulation (AM). AM is cheap and cheerful and was used for marine communication until 1982 when it was abandoned because it transmitted the modulated signal on either side of the carrier signal. In effect, the same information was transmitted twice and so occupied twice as much of the radio spectrum as necessary. This makes AM a double sideband (DSB) or A3E signal.

SINGLE SIDEBAND

Transmitting one sideband uses the radio spectrum more efficiently and if the carrier wave is also suppressed along with one of the sideband signals, so much the better for transmitting the carrier requires two-thirds of the transmission power with the remaining third equally divided between the two sidebands. Simple arithmetic shows that in DSB (A3E) signals, only a sixth of the transmitting power is used to carry the information sent, and of the 100 watts used, less than 20 watts carry your words.

On an SSB radio the unwanted sideband and the carrier wave are filtered out before the signal is amplified and passed to the antenna. When the signal is picked up, the receiving radio reinserts the carrier to allow the sideband signal to be demodulated and changed back into an audio signal. This halves the amount of the radio spectrum used and makes almost all the transmitting power available for carrying information. This is a single sideband suppressed carrier signal or J3E. DSB and SSB signals are not compatible

THE IONOSPHERE

The ionosphere was originally called the Heavyside layer and sometimes today this term is used to describe the E Layer, which is one of the four separate layers making up the ionosphere, each of which treats radio waves differently.

D LAYER

This is 30 to 50 miles above the earth and does not refract radio waves and absorbs those below 3MHz. It exists from just after sunrise to just before sunset when its disappearance allows signals in the MF band to reach the E Layer that can then reflect them and make ranges of up to 1000 miles possible for MF signals. This is why the MF band suddenly becomes busy at night and when you pick up Navtex signals far out at sea.

E LAYER

This is 60 to 90 miles above the earth. It is strongly ionised during the day and refracts radio waves up to around 8MHz. It is less strongly ionised at night when it refracts radio waves up to about 4MHz. There is

also the sporadic E Layer, small ionised 'clouds' which can have a life of several hours. Signals reflected from the E Layer have ranges up to around 1100 nautical miles.

F1 LAYER

This is 90 to 150 miles above the earth and is strongly ionised during the day when it refracts radio waves of 8–16MHz.

F2 LAYER

This is 150 to 250 miles above the earth and is strongly ionised during the day when it refracts radio waves of 16–30MHz.

During the night the F1 and F2 layers combine to form a single layer and this halves the maximum frequency that can be refracted; if during the day 16MHz band worked well for a particular station then during the night the best band to work the same station would probably be in the 8MHz band. Signals reflected from the F Layer have ranges up to around 1600–2100 nautical miles.

Fig 12 *The ionosphere by day.*

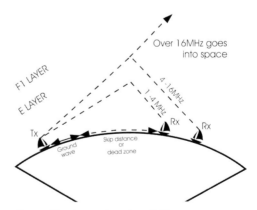

Fig 13 *The ionosphere by night.*

although during the transition period when SSB was introduced, a signal that could be received by both DSB and SSB receivers was introduced. This is the H3E mode and SSB sets would tune for the USB signal. H3E was mandatory for 2182MHz.

Bill knew that buying a short-wave receiver capable only of picking up commercial stations was a mistake. With an SSB receiver I could listen to the transatlantic ham radio nets, eavesdrop on the weather forecasts from Herb on *Southbound 2*, David on *Misteen* and listen to Mechanical Mike, the voice of NOAA weather. With the right computer programme, and a demodulator plugged into a laptop, I could also receive weatherfaxes.

Months later in St Martin I had the computer, the weatherfax programme and my own SSB receiver. All I needed to complete the package was a demodulator. I was given a wiring diagram but it looked like a cross between a crazy game of snakes and ladders and the Rosetta stone. Only then did it occur to me that, before I left, I should have acquired a better understanding of radios and electronics.

RECEIVING WEATHERFAX

A good weatherfax picture depends almost entirely on a good, noise-free signal. As a vehicle for receiving radio signals, yachts are at a disadvantage compared to land stations.

1 Fit the best antenna that you can find. A long wire antenna is not the best but it may be all that you can manage.
2 Fit an antenna tuner. This is next in importance to a good antenna.
3 Computers generate a lot of electronic noise and if this reaches the radio then it will degrade the signal. It can do this either through the antenna or the demodulator cable. To reduce the possibility of it reaching the antenna:
  • Keep the antenna and the computer as far apart as possible. This is difficult if you are working with a radio with a whip aerial two feet from the computer but if you can have the radio four feet away then the radio noise will halve: this type of interference falls away with the square of the distance.
  • Connect the antenna to the radio with a shielded cable. Try using 52 ohm 95% braid co-axial cable. Connect the antenna to the centre wire and the braid to the ground on the antenna jack plug that goes into the radio.
  • Turn off all electrical and electronic equipment except the computer, radio

and filament (tungsten) lights. GPS does not seem to interfere with reception.
4 To reduce the possibility of computer noise reaching the radio through the demodulator:
  • Wrap the connecting cable two or three times round a couple of ferrite beads. These can be bought in most radio shack type shops.
  • If this does not work then fit a 600 ohm audio transformer in the cable connecting the demodulator to the computer.
5 Turn off all filters on the radio such as tone, squelch, noise-blank.
6 Check you are using the correct sideband.
7 Check you have tuned the radio correctly. Remember that to receive weatherfax signals on an SSB receiver 1.7Hz must be subtracted from the frequency displayed on the receiver. If this is not done then although a signal will be received the tones will not be correct and the picture displayed degraded. Tune by ear first to make sure that you have a good, clear signal and then switch the signal to the computer. Buying a y-jack from Radio Shack means you can plug in an earphone and listen to the signal while still feeding the signal to the computer.
8 If the weatherfax station uses more than one frequency then find which one gives the best reception.

WEATHERFAXES

Weatherfax and weather information bulletins are transmitted on regular schedules by about 80 stations worldwide. If you do not have a dedicated weatherfax (WEFAX) receiver, the minimum equipment you need is an SSB receiver, a computer and a demodulator that turns the analogue radio signal into a digital signal that the computer will understand. You will also need a program for the computer to transform the signal into pictures or words.

Weatherfax charts are either an analysis of actual conditions or a forecast of future weather. Each chart takes between 8–10 minutes to receive and in remote areas they may be amongst your best, possibly the only, source of weather forecasting.

You can buy a proprietary weatherfax program and demodulator or you can download a suitable shareware program such as JVComm32 from the Internet. JVComm32 requires a computer that has, as a minimum, Windows 95, 16MB RAM, high or true colour graphics, Pentium processor operating at 100MHz and a 16-bit soundcard. The soundcard is important, for JVComm32 uses this as a demodulator. Some programs like HFFAX, JVFax and Hamcomm demand less sophisticated computers but all will require a separate demodulator.

Most weatherfax programmes also handle Navtex broadcasts but if you do not wish to run a computer all the time, inexpensive dedicated Navtex receivers are available. In theory, Navtex broadcasts have a maximum range of 300–400 miles. There are those who claim to have regularly received Navtex broadcasts in mid-ocean but this has probably been from sky wave signals at night.

Fashions in communications and electronics change quickly. By 1998 yachts carried SSB receivers as a matter of course; most carried HF transceivers and a few yachts had either Immarsat C or M satellite communications. Immarsat C is a radio telex service and Immarsat M behaves much like a normal telephone. Above the normal clamour of the Las Palmas yacht harbour was the constant trilling of cellphones, and in the emptiness of the Bahamas I met one yacht that had an Irridium telephone. 'It's really easy to use,' its proud owner said, insisting that I rang home from the middle of nowhere to prove his claims, but Irridium never recovered from the shock of calling north-east England and a few days later its satellites crashed and the system died.

No doubt all radios will eventually be replaced by a miniature widget that will be a radio, cellphone, GPS plotter, e-mail service, web browser and EPIRB but until this arrives there is a place for HF radio.

Enjoy the fun of Pedro's dinghy race before starting the serious business of the Atlantic challenge.

RADIO FREQUENCY INTERFERENCE (RFI)

RFI is when other onboard electrical or electronic equipment interferes with radio reception or transmission. The ideal solution is to turn off all other electrical equipment when using the radio but this is rarely feasible. Tracking down RFI is a slow, tedious task. The most common sources of RFI are:

- Alternators
- Electrical motors
- Fluorescent lights
- Rotating propeller shafts
- Televisions
- Radars
- Inverters
- Electronic logs and instrumentation

There may also be interference from the guardrails, rigging, other antennas and the ship's wiring.

The following hints may help you find sources of RFI.

- Try using a small portable transistor radio to track down the source of the RFI. The louder the interference the closer you are to its source.

- If the RFI is traced to an electrical motor (a very common cause) clean the motor's commutator and brushes. If the interference persists connect 05–1.0 micro-farad capacitors across each of the power leads and the ground (earth).
- If there is a humming from the radio when the engine is running see if it changes tone as you change engine speed. If so, the alternator is probably to blame. If the hum does not change pitch or if it is present when the engine is not running then suspect an inverter. Some inverters are very noisy (electronically) because they do not produce a true sine wave.
- Computers can generate a lot of electronic noise, which is fed back to the radio via the demodulator, and completely ruin reception of weatherfaxes. One solution is to fit ferrite chokes.
- When you find a source of RFI temporarily fit a 1 micro-farad capacitor between the suspect item of equipment and ground. If the RFI disappears fit the capacitor permanently.
- Keep radar scanners as far away as possible from radio antennas.

INSTALLING AN HF TRANSCEIVER

Installing an HF transceiver is more complicated than fitting a VHF set. A good ground plane (also called counterpoise) is vital. This means it must be earthed. An external keel or encapsulated solid keel can be used but best of all is a special, and expensive, external earthing plate fitted to the hull during the pre-cruise refit. If you are laying up your own boat then a copper mesh can be laid up between fibreglass layers to make a good ground plane or the mesh of a ferro-concrete hull can be used. It is also a good idea to ground all electrical equipment using the same wide copper tape used for the antenna. This will reduce the possibility of onboard interference to your signal.

ANTENNAS FOR HF

Ideally there should be a separate antenna for each frequency band. Instead it is usual to trick the backstay into behaving as if it is the correct length by an automatic tuning unit (ATU). This is sometimes referred to as an antenna coupler. The best are automatic and cover all frequencies but some meant for ham use, or older models, may only cover a limited number of frequencies and must be manually tuned.

If you are buying a second-hand set-up, check that the ATU covers all the frequencies you are likely to use. You may be told that it will 'broadband' on frequencies it does not cover. This sounds good but you are still putting out a lousy signal. If you use the

USING MARINE HF FREQUENCY BANDS

Different HF bands are capable of communicating over different distances at different times of day. Selecting the best band to listen or transmit can make all the difference to reception or transmission.

Take the ranges as a rough guide. Radio transmissions can be quirky and, with multiple skip, transmissions can be made and received over considerable distances.

Band	Range by Day	Likely Max	Range by Night	Likely Max	Remarks
2MHz	50–60	100	150–200	300	Often called LF Band
4MHz	150–200	300	800	1500	Dead by noon
6MHz	400		1000		
8MHz	300	500	1200	2000	At night stations closer than 500nm are in skip zone
12MHz	2000		1000	3000	
13MHz	2000		800		
16MHz	4000		unreliable		
17MHz	4000		unreliable		
22MHz					Daytime only worldwide band

Note: Onboard electrical equipment, especially inverters, can seriously degrade both radio reception and transmission and may need to be switched off when you are using the radio. Be alert for equipment like bilge pumps or refrigerators which may kick in during radio schedules.

backstay as an HF antenna then a spare 7–9 metre (23–30 foot) whip antenna should be carried in case you lose the mast.

If you have your HF transceiver professionally installed then, when the work is finished, ask the technician to make a radio check with a station at least 1000 miles away. His wattmeter may show 100 watts of power going out and his VSWR (Voltage to Standing Wave Ratio) declares that the forward power to the antenna is superb but a bad earth or poorly fitted ATU can make you sound like Donald Duck with a sore throat. Only after one or two distant stations have reported that they are receiving you loud and clear should you declare yourself satisfied and part with the cash.

MARINE VERSUS HAM RADIO

HF radios are normally sold either as ham sets or dedicated marine radios. Both receive on all frequencies but each will only transmit on the frequencies the authorities allocate for either marine or ham use. If you wish to transmit on both marine and ham frequencies you should have two transceivers, but the expense of two sets is avoided by modifying a radio to broadcast over all HF frequencies. This is a task for an expert.

Ham radio is not an alternative to a marine HF transceiver. It opens up the mobile ham chat nets and lets you speak directly to other yachts with ham radios and eavesdrop on almost everything travelling through the ether, but it will not handle GMDSS traffic or

COMPARING RADIOS

Type	Power	Range	Comments
Marine VHF	1 or 25 watts	Up to 30 miles line of sight. Varies with antenna height.	The workhorse of the sea. Every yacht has at least one set.
Marine SSB	150 watts	1000+ miles.	Ship-to-ship and some shore stations. Can handle e-mail and weatherfaxes.
Short-wave Receiver		Worldwide.	Can listen to Marine and Ham SSB broadcasts and receive weather faxes and Navtex.
Ham (Amateur Radio)	50–150 watts	Worldwide on HF bands. Two metre band corresponds to marine VHF.	Licence needed to operate. No music or profit making allowed.
Citizens Band	4 watts	Under 150 miles.	Different countries have different, non-compatible standards.

Prefixes

The prefixes *kilo* or *mega* allow the same frequency to be described in different ways. The frequency 4065kHz is 4065000 hertz and can also be written 4.065MHz.

One hertz (Hz) is one cycle per second
1000Hz is also 1 kilohertz (kHz)
1000kHz is also 1 megahertz (MHz) or one million hertz
1000MHz is also 1 gigahertz (GHz) or one thousand million hertz

transmit on any marine frequency. Ham sets tend to have more bells and whistles than the equivalent marine set and can be more demanding to operate, as you will have to remember which sideband you are using and if you are operating in simplex or duplex mode, and perhaps you will need to manually tune the ATU. On the plus side, not all ships and probably no yachts keep a full time watch on HF frequencies. They only switch on when it's time to join a net. But on the ham bands thousands of hams are straining their ears to pick up that elusive weak, long range (DX) signal. If you are in trouble and relying on the radio to bring help there is an argument that you stand a better chance of being heard on the ham bands.

OPERATORS' LICENCES

An operator's licence is necessary to transmit on any HF frequency. In the UK, using marine frequencies needs a Long Range Radio Operator's Certificate that comes from successfully completing a week-long course. It can be endorsed for satellite communications, which is useful if you install Immarsat C. An amateur licence is necessary to transmit on the HF ham frequencies. This can either be a full (send and receive 12wpm morse) or restricted (send and receive 5wpm morse) Class A licence. It is obtained by attending a night school course for 26 weeks starting in September, and in May taking a test administered by the City and Guilds Institute. A pass entitles you to apply for a

Class B licence and this is converted to a Class A licence by taking a separate morse test administered by the Radio Society of Great Britain. Different countries have their own, broadly similar, arrangements.

RADIO NETS

There are a number of radio nets that with an SSB receiver you may listen to and with an HF transceiver join in. Some nets are little more than chat lines carrying news and gossip but some give weather forecasts, which makes them very useful, particularly on passage. Nets can change their frequencies, times or even disappear but the ones listed in Appendix A should get you started.

In most Caribbean anchorages VHF channel 68 is the cruiser net used for ship-to-ship and ship-to-shore traffic. In some anchorages it is a completely informal arrangement, in others there is a regular morning net with a net controller and half an hour or so given over to news, advice,

weather and the nautical equivalent of garage sales. The cruiser net is where you call up the fuel barge, the water taxi, and the laundry, order a pizza and check when and where tonight's party is going to happen.

MAIL

I had been reluctant for Liz to send mail ahead to await my arrival. Not only might I change my mind and not go to my declared destination but I was never sure whether any or all of the advertised mail drops still existed. Instead I would arrive and then ask Liz to send my mail out to me. Mail drops are of two kinds: poste restante (General Delivery) and yacht clubs, marinas, bars and cafés that hold mail for yachts.

General delivery works well, but actually laying hands on your letters can be a bureaucratic nightmare and the only certainty is that the post office will be far from your boat.

Yacht clubs, marinas, bars and cafés are generally more conveniently located and less

The tranquil atmosphere of pontoon 10, the visitors' mooring at Las Palmas, where you can enjoy a last chilling-out session before the Atlantic crossing.

bureaucratic, but for them mail handling is a part-time sideline. Some provide excellent facilities, logging in every item of mail and ticking it off the list when handing it out. Some sling all the mail into a large cardboard box and leave everyone to rummage through hoping their turn has come. Marinas, bars and cafés can either go out of business or change hands and when that happens there is no knowing what will happen to any post that is waiting for you.

Whilst searching through several months of mail, accumulated for several hundred yachts, it occurred to me that it would be a good idea to train my correspondents to address all my mail in the same way. Simple is best: surname (or family name) with one initial and without titles or honorifics, boat name and then the address followed by the words 'To Be Called For' or 'To Await Arrival'. Unless you have a double-barrelled surname, the chances are your letter will be filed either under your name or your boat name. Including titles like Mr, Doctor, Captain and forenames simply increases the headings under which your mail can be filed.

TELEPHONES

The Canaries have good international telephone systems and calling home is no problem. It only takes cash to buy a phonecard. With some cards you insert the card into the telephone, with others you tap in a long series of numbers and then the number you want. The dialling sequence is the number to access the international network, usually 00 or 01, the country code and area code, then the number. In the Virgin Islands, boatphones can be hired for those who want the luxury of a telephone on their boat.

Every island has at least one mobile phone service that, if you are staying for any length of time, might be worth joining. Mobile phones are an area of communications that is expanding quickly.

EMAIL AFLOAT

Email Afloat is a radio telex service with an e-mail gateway and not all providers have the ability to handle attachments and some may limit the style of text you can use. Sending and receiving e-mails on board requires a communications device that includes e-mail as one of its facilities. This may be generic equipment or dedicated to one particular e-mail service or you can add bits and pieces to your HF transceiver to make it e-mail compatible.

Besides buying the necessary hardware costs can include annual fees, monthly fees, activation fees and a charge per character or per minute. The average e-mail is about 1000 characters. Check on the true (as opposed to advertised) coverage of the system and its availability, especially at busy times, otherwise you may find yourself in an area where coverage is poor or so limited that you wait forever to log on.

The following list of onboard e-mail providers is not exhaustive and will date as new systems come on line.

SATELLITE SYSTEMS

These are usually more reliable and easier to use than HF systems but normally you must use vendors' equipment.

Magellan GSC/Orbcomm
Uses low earth-orbiting satellites (LEOs) for two way e-mail communication. Both stations have to know which satellite to use. Equipment costs are between $1000–1500 plus $30 a month for ten messages of 500 characters and then one cent (US) per character. A text only system currently uses a Magellan GSC100 for e-mail and GPS positioning. Magellan also provides data and voice transmissions via the Inmarsat Systems through its World Phone.

Inmarsat A and B
The antennas used on these systems are generally too large for use on yachts.

Inmarsat C
Data and text only with built in GMDSS functions. Worldwide coverage. Can send e-mails to any address but only registered e-mail addresses can send to you. Equipment costs around $3000. There is no monthly charge but there is a charge of 0.5 cents per character and the unit must be left on all the time to receive weather alerts and distress calls.

Inmarsat M
This is more suitable for yachts than Immarsat A or B and offers voice and data transmissions but for yachts is being superseded by Inmarsat Mini-M.

Inmarsat Mini-M
Even more suitable for yachts and offers voice, data and text but no GMDSS functions or weather alerts. Used like a telephone for voice, data and fax messages. Links to computers via serial port or USB but no GMDSS distress, GPS or weather alert functions. There is a $2.90 per minute charge. The equipment costs from $5000 upwards.

HF SYSTEMS

HF systems are cheaper than satellite systems but marine SSB can, legally, only be used from a boat. Ham radio systems require a ham radio licence.

AirMail 2000
Interfaces with HF radios and provides a similar service to WinLink 2000.

CruiseEmail
Before combining with SeaMail, it had its own stations in Florida and Australia and plans to open more in Maryland and San Diego. Annual fee of $500 which gives 300 minutes a month and then a charge of 50 cents a minute but check this. Uses SeaMail software.

Globalstar
This has limited coverage and it is necessary to have both the boat and ground station visible to the satellite simultaneously. In November 2000 Globalstar opened a ground station in Puerto Rico, which should give reasonable coverage throughout the Caribbean.

Globe Wireless
Has worldwide coverage but nowadays concentrates on commercial shipping.

Marinenet
Has one station in Florida: annual fee allows five hours a month.

Message Center Inc
Provides HF SSB and VHF ship-to-shore communications and acts as a message centre for incoming calls via a pre-assigned telephone number. These messages are stored until you call in to retrieve them. SITOR (Simplex Teletype Over Radio) allows text to be sent and received over the Internet.

Pinoak Digital
Has one station based in New Jersey. Uses customised modem.

SailMail
A non-profit group with a yearly fee. Began with stations covering Hawaii, California, South Carolina and Australia but reported to be extending operations to cover Caribbean. Users are limited to 5–10 minutes a day.

SeaMail and CruiseEmail
These have combined to give worldwide coverage. Costs are based on 300 minutes a month over one year with additional time billed per minute.

WinLink 2000
This is for ham radio users as a radio mailbox (this is like an internet service provider), it handles text e-mails and attachments. Has 60 stations worldwide and is free.

E-MAIL

I had not thought about using e-mail until Roy from *Touchdown* expressed his amazement that anyone could live without an e-mail address, and dragged me off to the nearest Internet café, sat me down at a computer and signed me up. E-mail is a great way for the cruising tribe to keep in touch with each other and with home. E-mail is quicker than airmail and waits until you arrive wherever you are going. Using Internet cafés means that you do not need to have an internet service provider (ISP) and if you sign up with a free e-mail service such as Hotmail or Yahoo you only pay for the time on the café's machine. I had to sail into the Orinoco delta before I failed to find an Internet café.

If you have a laptop with a modem and your own ISP then it is possible to plug into a telephone socket and not use an Internet café but check that you are making a local call and not calling your ISP in England from Trinidad.

Companies like iPass and GRIC-Dial have schemes to access your e-mail for the price of a local call from anywhere (ashore) in the world.

A popular option is Pocketmail. This looks rather like a palm-size computer into which you type your e-mails and then go to a telephone, hold the Pocketmail to the handset to send and receive your e-mails. Pocketmail devices cost around $100 and there is an annual charge of $120 for unlimited usage in the USA via an 800 (free) phone number but messages are limited to 4000 characters and there are no attachments. If you have an HF transceiver then this can be set up to send and receive e-mail.

Preparations are never complete but when work eventually becomes an excuse to stay you know it is time to go. I made a last call home, told Liz I was off and I would not be in touch for a month, walked back to the pontoon, untied *Mintaka* and headed towards the breakwater to the accompaniment of sirens, hooters, bells and the good wishes of friends. What on earth was I doing?

8 The Trade Wind Route

My plan was to sail south-west until I met the Trades and then turn right and ride the winds until I reached Barbados. The cry of 'South till the butter melts' is replaced with 'sail for 25°N 25°W'. Either route takes you close to the Cape Verde Islands and I marked them as a bolthole. I had no intention of stopping en route but when plans start to fall apart it looks better to announce alternative arrangements than to appear as if you are fleeing in fright.

This is the route which has been followed by sailing vessels since 1492 but there are other ways west. I could have sailed direct from Europe on the cold, hard northern route that would have brought me high on the eastern seaboard of the USA. It means sailing far enough north to catch the easterly winds blowing round the top of the depressions coming in from the Atlantic. Even then much will be to windward, beyond the ice limits and into the cold, foggy waters of the Labrador Current. It is popular with racers who sacrifice comfort for speed. For those interested in this route, Phil Weld looked at the weather records over 20 years and concluded that the centre of the fiercest storms lay to the north of 45°N 35°W. A warmer non-stop route is to sail south through the Azores or you can pause at Madeira and then head for the Caribbean but both of these are only variations on the Trade Wind Route.

Although most boats aim for the Lesser Antilles and a few for the Bahamas, it is not mandatory to make directly for the Caribbean. Some yachts head south to Dakar and then sail west, via the Cape Verde Islands, for the Caribbean. Others make for Brazil, French Guyana, Suriname or Guyana on the mainland of South America before cruising northwards for Trinidad and the Lesser Antilles.

Halfway between the Cape Verde Islands and Barbados the nearest land is mainland Brazil or the Ilha do Fernando de Noronha. From there it is a short cruise to the Atol das Rocas and on to the mainland of South America. As the Antilles become more and more developed, spending some of the season cruising the South American coast will become more attractive.

The greatest danger of the classic route is heading west early into the calms of the Azores High. In winter this lurks west of the Canaries and sailing south-west until you are firmly in the Trades adds miles but proves quicker.

Since leaving Falmouth I had averaged 80 miles a day but according to the pilot chart for December the winds were always north-easterly and the Canaries Current would carry me south and west until the North Equatorial Current picked me up and added eight to ten miles to my daily run, or between 220–240 free miles for the entire passage – three days off my expected seatime. It would be downhill sailing in the sun, a milk run. *Mintaka* would romp along. I calculated 30 days to Barbados and dreamt of 25, but to be safe I allowed 35.

This ignored the teachings of Cowards Anonymous. Instead of avoiding doom by anticipating disaster I was planning for the best and assuming all would go according to plan. More to the point I was overlooking the Horse Latitudes.

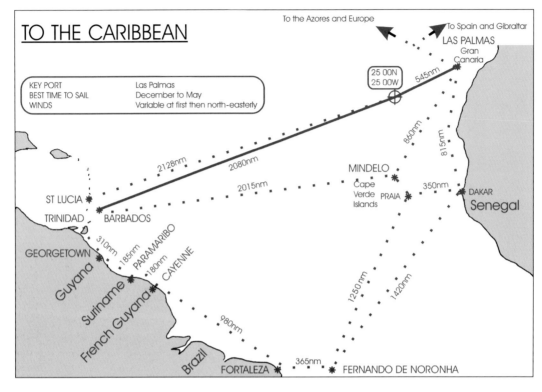

Fig 14 *Las Palmas to Barbados.*

The Trades may be found as far north as Madeira but in the winter they follow the sun south and the space they once occupied is leased to light, variable winds called the Horse Latitudes. Some years these reach hundreds of miles south of the Canaries. In the old days they would see salty, shellbacked skippers throwing horses overboard when passages grew long and water and fodder ran short. A week out of Las Palmas I began to believe that it would be quicker on horseback.

enough for them to be decently dashed. With yesterday's rubbish lying alongside there is always a strong sense of going nowhere. No wonder the ancient mariner went mad.

Exhausted by 30 hours of wind-chasing I took the sails down, silenced the rattles with towels and slept, to discover that I travelled as far in the 8 hours of sleep as in 8 hours of effort. It was a useful lesson. After that, when I ran into a calm I rolled away the sails, lashed everything down and took to my bunk with a good book until the wind returned.

HANDLING CALMS

Days and nights were spent becalmed or chasing zephyrs with a useful working life of minutes. It is rare for an absence of wind to be accompanied by a flat sea. There is always swell enough for the boom to sway, the sails to flap and anything loose to rattle, roll or creak. Nor are calms absolute. Soft breezes momentarily fill the sails and raise hopes high

TROPICAL REVOLVING STORMS

Once, for variety, the barometer dropped 12 points in 24 hours. The received wisdom is that a fall of 5 points below the seasonal average comes with a gold-plated promise of a full-grown, genuine tropical revolving storm. It is unusual for these to be part of the Christmas festivities but bad fairies and bad pennies enjoy turning up when least

Expect to experience some big seas on your passage across the Atlantic; you will find that you will hone your weather forecasting skills and become an avid listener to radio bulletins.

expected. It would be an understatement to describe my reaction as helpless terror.

From a peak in the 1940s and 1950s, hurricane activity fell during the 1960s through to the 1990s. Since the mid-1990s, activity has picked up and some experts believe that the early part of the 21st century will bring more hurricanes and that more of these will be of the most severe class.

In the tropics, shallow westward-moving low pressure troughs are called 'easterly waves'. They bring overcast skies and showers with the possibility of thunderstorms and strong squalls. If an easterly wave develops a closed circulation it appears on synoptic charts with one or more closed isobars and is called a tropical depression and has winds of force 7 or less. In the right conditions a tropical depression grows into a tropical storm with winds between force 8–11 and perhaps a hurricane with winds over force 11.

HANDLING TROPICAL REVOLVING STORMS

The safest way of dealing with a tropical revolving storm is to declare a 200 mile exclusion zone around its centre. Observing this should bring nothing worse than a force 6.

If you are at sea and it looks likely you will approach closer than 200 miles you have two options. The first is to put out a Mayday call immediately. Hopefully, this will be heard and a vessel diverted to take off you and your crew. It is unlikely that they will attempt to salvage your boat and may even deliberately sink it to prevent it becoming a hazard to shipping. This option must be taken early to allow time for a vessel to reach you before the weather becomes too bad to make abandoning ship dangerous.

The second option is to ride it out. This is the choice of last resort and not to be undertaken if any other option is available. Your first task is to put as much searoom between you and the storm as possible. If you

STEERING CLEAR OF STORMS

A weather forecast is received telling of a storm bearing 155°T range 365nm. It is travelling on a course of 235°T at 12 knots. You are steering 285° at 5 knots.

    You want to know the best course to steer to avoid the storm and how close it will approach (CPA). The answers may be found graphically or mathematically.

BEST AVOIDANCE COURSE

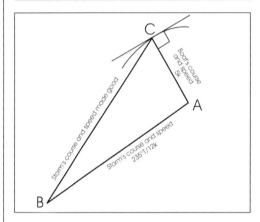

Graphic Solution

1 Draw a line AB at a suitable scale to represent the course and track of the storm.
2 From A draw an arc on the same scale with a radius equal to your boat's speed.
3 From a tangent to this arc draw a perpendicular to meet AB at C.

In this vector triangle
AB represents the storm's course and speed
BC represents the storm's course and speed made good
AC represents the boat's course and speed
Angle A represents the best avoidance course.

Mathematical Solution
Angle A = 90 – Sin boat speed/storm speed
       = 90 – Sin 5/12
       = 65°

This angle is relative to the storm's course and must be converted to 360° notation to give a course to steer when it gives a course of 300°T.

Storm's speed made good = BC = Sin A x storm speed
           = Sin 65 x 12
           = 10.9 knots

CPA

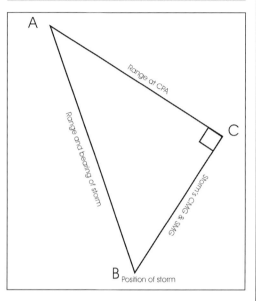

Graphic Solution

1 Draw a line AB at a suitable scale representing the distance bearing of the storm from your present position at point A.
2 Through A draw a line on the same scale representing the reciprocal of the best avoidance course.
3 From B drop a perpendicular to meet this line at C.

In this vector triangle
AC represents the range of the storm at the CPA.
BC represents the distance made good by the storm to reach the CPA.
C represents the CPA.

Mathematical Solution
AC   = Sin B x range of storm
       = Sin 50 x 365
       = 280nm

BC   = Sin A x range of storm
       = Sin 40 x 365
       = 235nm

As the SMG of the storm is 10.9 knots then it will arrive at the CPA in about 21 hours 30 minutes.

Note Storms do not always follow forecasts, tracks or timetables and calculations must be updated to reflect the changing situation.

cannot win enough searoom to avoid the storm, try to place your vessel in the navigable semi-circle where the winds are least. If a hurricane is travelling due west at 10 knots then to the north of its centre its speed of advance is added to the windspeed and a 70-knot wind feels like 80 knots; to the south of its centre it is subtracted with the apparent wind therefore 60 knots. As wind force increases as the square of the windspeed, this 20-knot difference could be important. Even so, the difference between navigable and dangerous semi-circles is relative. In both there are violent and strong winds and extraordinarily dangerous seas.

Once the wind is backing then you are in the navigable semi-circle and the traditional advice is to run with the wind on your starboard quarter, altering course as the wind continues to back. If there is insufficient room to run then it may be necessary to choose between the lesser of two evils and enter the dangerous semi-circle to avoid the eye.

In the dangerous semi-circle, the traditional advice is to heave-to on the starboard tack, altering course as the wind veers. If the wind remains constant or backs it is likely that you are in the direct path of the eye or possibly in the navigable semi-circle and, as before, you should run with the wind on the starboard quarter. There is some evidence that the use of parachute sea-anchors is helpful in extreme conditions, particularly if you do not have the searoom to run before the weather.

Encountering and surviving a hurricane at sea will take careful and consummate seamanship leavened by a heavy dose of good fortune. It will require estimating the relative position of the storm, using information gleaned both from weather forecasts and by frequent and meticulous observations of the wind direction under extraordinarily difficult conditions, in order to reach safer waters as soon as possible.

DOWNBURSTS

A downburst is caused by a thunderstorm at its nastiest. Warm water under a thunderhead cloud (cumulonimbus) creates an updraft that displaces cold air as it rises. The cold air drops, accelerating as it goes until it hits the sea and bursts. This is the microburst phase where the winds can reach over 100 knots and it covers an area of around three miles in diameter. Once the microburst phase is complete the winds decrease to around that of a normal ferocious squall and can spread out over a much wider area. Downbursts may occur without a preceding microburst.

The good news is that they are over in less than ten minutes although a single thunderstorm may produce a sequence of downbursts lasting over an hour; the bad news is that they cannot be predicted. It is reckoned that the loss of the *Pride of Baltimore* near Puerto Rico in 1986 was due to a microburst. Eyewitnesses reported that the ship was blown over and sank in less than two minutes.

THE HURRICANE SEASON

Tropical storms and hurricanes generally come between June to November with activity peaking in September and October. Hurricanes normally originate closer to the Cape Verde Islands than the Caribbean, travel west at about ten knots until they make a landfall between Martinique and St Martin and turn (or recurve) north towards the American seaboard, increasing their speed to between 15–20 knots. Exhausted by trashing the Caribbean and the eastern seaboard they head for Europe as a temperate, but vigorous, low pressure system.

Pay close attention to reports of all storm systems, tropical or otherwise. In coastal and offshore waters a storm 400 miles away can nearly always be ignored even if it is coming at you at 20 knots. Long before it arrives you are either safely in port or diverted to a safe harbour. When ocean cruising there may be just enough time to get out of its way. When

This coaster was blown ashore at Portsmouth on Dominica during a hurricane.

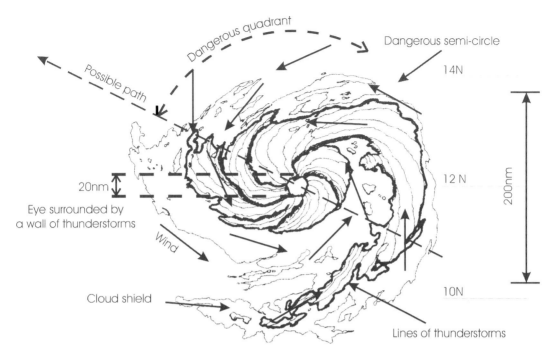

Fig 15 *The structure of a revolving storm.*

you hear a storm warning your first act should be to plot its point of closest approach and relax only when you are satisfied you will miss its worst weather.

STRUCTURE OF A HURRICANE

A typical depression in temperate latitudes will have a central pressure of around 960mbs and a diameter of 1200 nautical miles. Tropical revolving storms have a similar central pressure but a diameter of between 400–500 miles. A steeper pressure gradient not only brings stronger winds but they increase in strength differently. In a temperate depression the winds increase steadily from about 15 knots on its outskirts to 50 knots at the centre. In a tropical revolving storm, winds from the perimeter increase slowly to reach gale force about 125 miles from the centre, and then increase more and more rapidly until the eye wall is reached, when they will suddenly fall to about 15 knots. Once the eye has passed then they will just as suddenly return at full strength.

A tropical wave can grow to a hurricane in less than 12 hours. Fortunately hurricanes rarely arrive unannounced. Like most bullies they give warning of their approach. Weather information services begin broadcasting frequent warnings by radio (commercial and marine bands), TV and internet. Should you miss these then signs of an approaching tropical revolving storm include:

- In the open sea, swell is pushed ahead of the storm.
- Cirrus clouds form in bands pointing towards the storm centre followed later by alto-stratus, then broken cumulus and scud carrying rain squalls.
- If after being corrected for latitude, temperature and diurnal variation the barometer is 3mb below the average then a tropical revolving storm is likely: 5mb below the mean and it is a promise. In the tropics the greatest changes in barometric pressure come from diurnal variation. At 10 o'clock in the morning and evening the barometer will rise a point or two and at 4

o'clock morning and afternoon it will drop a couple of points. A slowly falling barometer with the diurnal variation still evident means the storm centre is 120–400 miles away. If the diurnal variation is masked by the falling barometer then the storm centre is within 120 miles. If you do not note the hourly barometric pressure think about investing in an electronic barometer, which records at least 24 hourly readings.

- Any change in wind speed or direction should be regarded with suspicion.

IN THE TRADES

Small, isolated cumuli looking like the outpourings of a steam engine are meant to be a sure sign of the Trades. For days I was surrounded by Puffing Billy clouds without a breath of wind in sight. If a wind did appear it was from the south. It was so perverse I came to believe that the Trades were a myth. The temptation to flash up the engine was almost irresistible. But to what end? I had fuel for about 100 miles, no distance at all, and afterwards I would be out of fuel and probably still in the same weather pattern. No, we were making slow progress and at some stage the weather had to improve.

I finally met the Trades just south of 20°N. At first they were so shy that I was worried that my presence would scare them away. Very quietly I raised the spinnaker as a sign of my good intentions and kept it flying for the next 21 hours until the wind had gained sufficient confidence to blow *Mintaka* along under the more traditional rig of boomed-out jibs.

I took stock; 12 days of calms, headwinds and one gale were making it a long drawn-out trip. I ought to let the folks at home know that I would be delayed. I looked around for the nearest telephone and, in accordance with previous arrangements, made for the Cape Verdes and the island of Sao Vicente. It was three days before I arrived.

HURRICANES

In the northern hemisphere, the official hurricane season is from 1 June to 30 November each year. Worldwide there are about 85 tropical storms a year and 45 of these will grow into hurricanes or typhoons. Oral accounts of tropical revolving storms in the Caribbean go back to the 16th century. These concentrate on extreme storms whose severity made them part of the local folklore. Detailed records go back just over 100 years. Between 1886 and 2000 there were 997 tropical storms, an average of nine each year; about six become hurricanes and two intense or severe hurricanes.

In this period there was at least one tropical storm or hurricane each year, usually more. The worst year was 1995 with 19 tropical storms/hurricanes, 1968 had 18 and 1887 had 17 tropical storms/hurricanes.

The average for the 40 years between 1950 to 1990 is:

Named Storms	9.9
Named Storm Days	46.9
Hurricanes	5.8
Hurricane Days	23.7
Intense Hurricanes	2.2
Intense Hurricane Days	4.7

The official hurricane season is 183 days. Taking the 40-year average as 100%, 1999 hurricane activity rated 160% with 77 named storm days.

CAUSES

Hurricane activity has been linked to La Niña, which encourages hurricane formation, rather than El Niño, which discourages it. Their formation is also associated with high sea surface temperatures and high salinity in the North Atlantic. This phenomena is called the Atlantic Conveyor Belt and was strong from the 1930s to the late 1960s, a time of high hurricane activity. The belt was weak between 1900–1925 and 1970–1994 when hurricane activity was less intense.

Recent studies showed that the probability of hurricanes in the Gulf of Mexico and the Caribbean increases fourfold when the winds blow from the west in the Eastern Pacific Ocean. This is the Madden-Julian oscillation and it occurs every 30 to 60 days. It starts in the Indian Ocean and travels across the Pacific resulting in a shift from easterly to westerly winds.

A further complication to a simplistic explanation of the cause of hurricanes is the stratospheric equatorial winds; easterly stratospheric equatorial winds are reckoned to discourage the formation of hurricanes.

Since the mid-1990s activity has picked up and some experts believe that the early part of the 21st century means more hurricanes and more in the most severe class. From a study of marsh sediments covering the last 5000 years Kam-bui Liu of Louisiana State University argues that the last 1000 years has been a period of mild hurricane activity and that the next millennium will bring more frequent and stronger storms.

NAMING HURRICANES

In the 1930s an Australian forecaster, using the names of unpopular politicians, began naming hurricanes. Between 1950 and 1952 the phonetic alphabet was used to name Caribbean hurricanes. From 1953 they were given the saint days of islands, later they were christened with female names and nowadays hurricanes are given male and female names in alternate years.

POWER OF HURRICANES

It is difficult to meaningfully express a hurricane's power. Satellite pictures show that they are not the neat arrangement of winds and isobars popular in illustrations but a whirling mass of ferocious winds, thunderstorms and torrential rain. In a single day even a modest hurricane will produce as much energy as most European countries use in a year. There can be 36 inches of rain (914mm) in 24 hours. In 1928 one hurricane dropped two and a half billion gallons of water on Puerto Rico. In Deshaies on Guadeloupe, cement mooring blocks in 40 feet of water were thrown onto the beach. In 1970 one hurricane killed 300,000 people in Bangladesh. Barometric pressure in the hurricane's eye can be less than 914mb (27 inches of mercury). Any right thinking yachtsman will consider meeting a force 10 storm a very serious proposition. The wind force (not speed) in a hurricane is 12 to 16 times as great.

SAFFIR/SIMPSON HURRICANE SCALE

A tropical depression is a tropical cyclone with one or more closed isobars and maximum sustained surface winds of under 34 knots. In a tropical storm the maximum sustained surface wind increases to 63 knots and it is given a name. In a hurricane the winds are from 64 knots upwards.

Category	Winds (knots)	Winds (mph)	Winds (m/s)	Typical centre pressure (Mbs)	Damage (ashore)
1	65.2–82.6	75–95	33.5–42.5	Above 980	Minimal
2	83.4–95.6	96–110	42.9–49.2	965–979	Moderate
3	96.5–113	111–130	49.6–58.1	945–964	Extensive
4	114–135	131–155	58.6–69.3	920–944	Extreme
5	Over 135	Over 155	Over 69.3	Under 920	Catastrophic

Tornadoes are measured on the Fujita scale ranging from FO with winds under 117kph (63.2 knots/42.5m/s) to F5 where the winds are over 512kph (276 knots/142m/s).

SITTING IT OUT

When the barometer took a dive I was stuck between the Canaries and the Cape Verde Islands. Apart from checking stowage arrangements and having a meal there was little to do but wait. Not only was the hurricane season officially over but I reckoned that any decent tropical revolving storm should form up west of my position and then march west. If so, then I was already moving towards its safe sector. I should only touch its fringes, but if I was wrong then Africa and Cap Blanc looked horribly close. I could not help remembering that I was not far from where the *Medusa*, of raft fame, went aground. I banished the thought and told myself that this storm was going to obey the rules and go west, but theories exist to be disproved so I was relieved to meet nothing worse than two days of south-westerly force 5–6.

Even so it was on the limits of *Mintaka*'s windward performance with a troubled sea expressing its frustrations by striking out violently in all directions. Fierce squalls took advantage of the confusion to launch frequent sneak attacks. The force of their blows laid *Mintaka*, under bare poles, over and the torrential rain that came with them closed down visibility and hammered the sea until it took on a flat, grey, burnished pewter sheen. It was an impressive performance.

It is usual to describe waves breaking at sea as 'snarling' or 'roaring', but from close and prolonged observation I can reveal that their snarls and roars are the contented purring of a well-fed kitten. The true breaking wave comes straight at you like a jet fighter making a low pass with its afterburners on overtime. And when the black of the night merges with the dark of the sea the sound is one of life's eye-opening, mouth-drying, heart-stopping experiences. Then it hits you.

THE CAPE VERDE ISLANDS

Uninhabited before the Portuguese arrived in the 15th century, the Cape Verdes are culturally as well as geographically closer to Africa than Europe. Unknown and unspoilt by tourism they are well worth a visit. Mindelo is Sao Vicente's only town and the archipelago's second largest. It is home to 50,000 people and sprawls around the north end of Porto Grande, the deep bay that provides a splendid, natural anchorage for visiting yachts. Its only drawbacks are the squalls dropping down from the surrounding hills and the crowd of boat boys offering to watch your dinghy, fetch water, fuel and shop every time you go ashore. It is off-putting but it is the only living they have and they work hard for whatever you pay them.

ATLANTIC BOAT BOYS

This was my first encounter with boat boys. I had crept in during the night and anchored off what was once the yacht club. Waking up late I was staring at the mass of people on the shore when a dinghy came alongside and its occupant introduced himself as Pedro, my boat boy. As I slowly absorbed this information the throng on the shore grew quiet listening for my reply. The penny dropped. This was a city of unemployed boat boys. 'No thanks,' was not going to bring me peace. Pedro and I sealed our deal by shaking hands. I was an employer.

There is almost no industry in Sao Vicente. Before winning independence from Portugal, the colonial civil service provided many jobs for the people of the Cape Verdes, as did the shipping lines. Nowadays, jobs are scarce and income from expatriates, once a mainstay of the economy, is close to zero. For the want of anything better and the chance of earning a few escudos, young men gather on the beach to wait for passing yachts.

Pedro explained that to improve his chances as a boat boy he had learned English from the crews of yachts that employed him. Having expensively acquired six words of French and three of Spanish I was humbled.

Whenever I went ashore Pedro was there to guard my dinghy, fetch water and fuel or point me towards the best cafés and bars. He took my laundry and brought it back not just washed but ironed. If Pedro was not around when I wanted to return to *Mintaka* the other boat boys would set up a hue and cry until he appeared clutching the dinghy's oars. I never learned where he took the oars.

Hopes of restocking with fresh food in Mindelo were dashed by a wall-sized cartoon at the entrance to the market. As far as I could make out it warned of the existence of cholera and advised washing all fruit and vegetables in bleach before eating them. There is a supermarket but, compared to Las Palmas, it is small, pricey and with limited stock. There is also a small open-air market but each day as the local fishing boats returned I made a point of negotiating my share of their catch.

Porto Santo and Sao Vicente both hold echoes of earlier times and are looking to tourism to boost their economies. By 1999 Porto Grande had the beginnings of a marina, yacht services were starting to develop, and there were rumours that in future ARC boats would pause on Sao Vincente on their way to St Lucia.

CAPE VERDE ISLANDS TO BARBADOS

When the Trades blow across the Cape Verdes they are squeezed down the channel between Sao Vicente and the neighbouring island of San Antao. This speeds them up and their accompanying swell steepens and ricochets between the islands creating a lumpy, disgruntled sea while the sand carried by the wind from Africa reduces visibility to a handful of miles.

I learned this at first hand as I left the shelter of Porto Grande. It destroyed my newly refreshed morale. Being rattled around for a month or more covered in Saharan sand held little attraction but second thoughts were academic. Like a small child going down a helter-skelter there was no going back. I was totally committed so I closed my eyes, and went.

Quirky signs like these are common-place in the Caribbean; it emphasises how you should be aware of, and observe, local customs and laws.

In the Trades, wind strength can blow from a force 2 to a 6 in the time it takes to make a cup of coffee but as long as the following seas remain regular, life is fine. Problems, and discomfort, come from seas that run across the grain. They always produce horrendous rolling and, given the slightest encouragement, slap *Mintaka* so hard that she would snap her sails loudly, dig her stern in and spin round in a flurry of spray. This once went on for 36 disheartening hours. But this was balanced by days and nights of easy rolling seas and sailing down the glitter of moonshine under a star-filled sky.

Be prepared for set-backs to morale. I celebrated passing the halfway mark. For the first time *Mintaka* and I had sailed 1000 miles non-stop. Surely that deserved a glass or two? Next morning dawn revealed the ocean looking the same as ever and far from arriving somewhere I felt stuck in the middle of nowhere forever. There is a similar feeling in long distance running. It is called the wall. The only remedy is to shove the wall aside.

Towards evening I threw the fishing line out in the hope of fish for tea but when I hauled in the line, my favourite lure and some feet of line had vanished. Probably just as well as sharing the cockpit with any fish capable of snapping a 60lb breaking strain line would have been an interesting challenge. It certainly would have been upset and it is a moot point who would have had the first bite. I had to smile. Life was back to normal.

Flying fish need no invitation to leap aboard. Most mornings saw one or two on deck. They are curious creatures. They pop out of a wave and with their translucent wings extended and sparkling in the sun they soar across the sea. Taking advantage of every eddy in the wind they rise and fall with the waves for a respectable 30 or 40 metres before making a splash landing; sometimes flying solo or in squadrons. For the first half of the trip Madeiran Terns skimmed the waves and all the way across, the aristocratic Bosunbird would circle around looking down its beak at *Mintaka* as though unsure at what it saw sailing on its ocean. Apart from one container ship that passed 5 or 6 miles away, that was the total company that I had during the crossing. I read a lot and listened to the radio.

TRADE WIND RIG

I used an old, baggy jib to run under twin jibs. It still had its hanks and I considered hanking it onto an old forestay (carried as a spare) and shackling it and the jib to the spinnaker halyard so that I had the illusion of twin forestays. I abandoned this as too complicated and set the old jib flying from the spinnaker halyard and rolled away some of the genoa so that both sails were about the same sail area. Both were poled out and once clear of the Cape Verdes, sail handling rarely rose above deciding on one jib or two. Invariably I got it wrong. I would fly both and cower in terror as we raced along in a near continuous surf. This produced the best day's run of 115 miles but if I took one sail down then within minutes we would be barely moving.

True decadence arrived when I discovered that if I wanted only one jib then I rolled away the genoa, letting the pole go forward until it was time to pull the genoa out and once again carry twin jibs. Both operations were carried out in minutes standing in the main hatch.

Real yachtsmen rush along under spinnakers or cruising chutes but twin jibs will keep you moving well with the bonus that they are controllable, work with self-steering, and rolling the genoa halves the sail area in seconds. Their main drawback is that they take time to set up or take down and a decision to change to another rig must be made well in advance.

LATITUDE SAILING

Between the Cape Verde Islands and the Caribbean it is latitude sailing on a grand scale. Barbados is 2000 miles west but less than two hundred miles south of Mindelo. Most nights, once I had found the Big Dipper, then Polaris, low on the horizon, shone out like a beacon.

For trade wind sailing I found that twin jibs will keep you moving well in the Trades and they are controllable and can be reduced quickly if necessary. Their disadvantage is that they take time to set up or take down so a change of rig has to be planned.

Fig 16 *The polar clock. In the northern hemisphere you can pretend that the Pole Star is the centre of a clock face and the Little Dipper (Ursa Minor), or Kochab, is the hand. Imagine one line running north-south through Polaris and another line running east-west. These are the reference points for your clock but they cannot represent 3, 6, 9 or 12 o'clock because Kochab circles Polaris anticlockwise. Find Kochab and note its position relative to Polaris and look at your watch. This is your start time and for every hour, Kochab will move 15 degrees anticlockwise. Looking at your watch may be cheating but it is the easiest way I know of calibrating this 'clock' and after a couple of nights you can probably manage without your watch.*

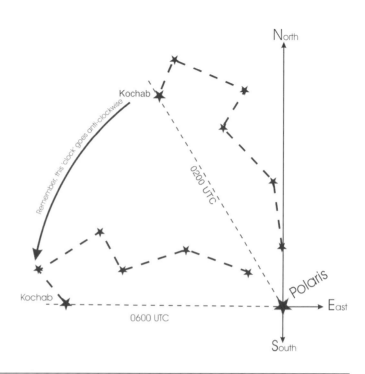

Polaris makes a 1° circle around true north and, with minimal corrections, its altitude is your latitude. As a rough guide, a line joining the star at the end of the Big Dipper's handle to the Pole Star becomes the hand of a clock. When it points to twelve o'clock, 1° is added to the Pole Star's altitude to obtain latitude, at six o'clock, 1° is subtracted and at three and nine o'clock there is no correction. It is reckoned that below 10°N Polaris is too low for navigational use (see Fig 16).

It was fun to sit in the cockpit, estimate the Pole Star's altitude and correction and then compare my answer to the GPS position. I knew that I ought to allow for refraction and height of eye but there was also a more serious purpose to this game. If all else failed could I use the Pole Star to find Barbados? I like to think so. Each evening the Pole Star's altitude was more or less what I expected, although I could never exclude the possibility of a self-fulfilling prophecy for I knew the answer before I started.

After 19 days reading material was running thin and I was keen for a change in my diet of

BBC World Service. A hunt through the radio spectrum brought in the Voice of Barbados Radio. It was firm evidence that I was somewhere close to land. Since the water was holding up well I filled the solar shower and had a bath.

ARRIVAL IN BARBADOS

Land always pops up when your back is turned. On my first crossing in *Mintaka*, just as I settled down for afternoon tea in the cockpit there it was, a whale-like hump breaking the horizon. Night fell and the island became a jewel flecked with pinpoints of light topped by the fireflies of aircraft taking off and landing on the south of the island.

Needham Point marks the entrance to Carlisle Bay, in the south-west corner of Barbados. Once it was safely astern, I handed the sails. We motored the last few cables through the darkness into the anchorage until the sound of surf breaking on the invisible beach cracked my nerve and I threw the anchor overboard. The Trades pushed us back. We stopped.

Apart from a few hours in uncomfortable cross seas, it had been wonderful downhill sailing. In just over 21 days we had sailed 2000 miles. For the last 14 days we had averaged 100 miles a day. On the daily radio nets I heard others talk of being struck by fierce and sudden squalls but I only saw dark shadows on the horizon. Trade wind sailing was a piece of cake. Nothing to it. I looked around identifying familiar yachts. There were only two questions. Where was the bar and when was happy hour?

THE *MARGO* EXPERIENCE

It was so different when I crossed on *Margo* and it was largely my own fault. In Las Palmas Peter Forthmann told me that I had fitted my Windpilot self-steering gear wrongly and it needed to be modified to deliver its full power. I should have listened – he had designed the gear. But it had worked well so far as fitted and since I had better ways of spending my time I ignored his advice. It was not so much pride going before a fall – rather my ego tripping me up and jumping all over me.

Shortly after I sailed, the weather went pear-shaped: 17 days out of a 35-day passage to Barbados were spent in gale force winds or near continuous squalls of 35 to 45 knots and (very) occasionally higher. If that were not enough there was a vicious cross sea of two, sometimes three, wave trains that gave a good impression of the inside of a washing machine.

The way I had it rigged was asking too much of the self-steering gear, which never held a course for more than a few moments. When it did work it sawed through steering lines in minutes and I spent hours hanging over the stern reeving new lines.

In a fit of carelessness I threw one spinnaker pole overboard and although I tried using the main boom as a substitute, attempts at running under twin jibs were never successful. Progress was slow as I zigzagged over the ocean looking for the Trades. It was

a time of unmitigated discomfort that took my morale to depths I did not know it possessed. It was little comfort to discover, much later, that others had suffered as much or more than me. One boat had been damaged in a knockdown and another laid flat for over half an hour in a squall.

ELECTRICAL STORMS

I ran into an electrical storm that lit up the night for hours and induced a state of mindless fright. It is no fun sitting under the highest object for miles around watching the gods see who can throw the brightest and loudest thunderbolt. At one stage it was all happening less than half a mile away and just when I thought it could not be any more frightening I noticed that the antennas were glowing bright green.

A lightning strike, even a near miss, can fry electronics and destroy your compass, leaving you playing blind man's buff. A really bad strike can blow out chainplates, skin fittings and keel bolts. The usual advice is to protect portable electronic equipment such as the handheld VHF and spare GPS by placing it in the oven as a poor man's Faraday box. I carried the handheld VHF and GPS in the crash bag and I have never heard of anyone abandoning ship carrying an oven. Not having an oven I escaped this dilemma.

When I reached Barbados I scrounged an old ammunition box and filled it with GPS, torch, compass and spare batteries so that I had enough equipment to navigate and communicate if I lost the main electrics. Ammo boxes are not only made of metal but they are tolerably waterproof. It is worth giving lightning protection some thought for at certain times of the year there are frequent electrical storms off the Venezuelan coast and the eastern seaboard of the USA.

The other lesson I learnt from this second crossing was that in blue-water sailing there is no such thing as local knowledge, and the classic Trade Wind Crossing is not always a milk run.

9 Caribbean Cruising

The northern boundary of the Caribbean is a line running from Cuba through the Bahamas to the Virgin Islands. The Lesser Antilles is its eastern border and it is bounded in the south and west by South America, Panama and Central America. The 100 mile wide Yucatán Channel between the Yucatán Peninsula and Cuba leads to the Gulf of Mexico, which is generally considered separately. The name Caribbean is derived from the Carib Indians inhabiting the islands when the Spanish arrived.

CARIBBEAN GEOGRAPHY

The Greater Antilles is geologically part of the Central and South American mountain ranges where peaks of over 2000 metres are common. The Caribbean's highest point is Pico Duarte (10 417 feet/3175 metres) in the Dominican Republic. Much of the Lesser Antilles lies on a volcanic ridge and many islands have active volcanoes. Other islands in the Lesser Antilles are coral and limestone. The highest point of the Lesser Antilles is Morne Disblotins (4747 feet/1447 metres) on Dominica. Elsewhere heights rarely exceed 3900 feet or 1200 metres. Geologically the ABC Islands and Trinidad are part of South America and the low lying, coral and limestone of the Bahamas is related to the Florida peninsula.

Currents in the Caribbean are dominated by the North and South Equatorial Currents. The South Equatorial Current sweeps round the top of South America, joins the North Equatorial Current, and runs along the Venezuelan and Central American coasts towards the Yucatán Channel where it splits. Some of this current takes a tour of the Gulf of Mexico as the Loop Current before rejoining the main stream, and an offshoot of the North Equatorial Current runs along the north coasts of Puerto Rico and Cuba as the Antilles Current to catch up with the main current as it rushes out through the Florida Straits as the Gulf Stream.

Currents are not overly important in the Eastern Caribbean where most passages are north-south but for travelling west to east or east to west they play an important role in route planning. The tidal range is low and except for entrances through reefs or in narrows it is usually ignored.

Your first port of call in the Caribbean introduces you to bureaucracy in the sun. Arriving in Barbados you go to the Deep Water Harbour. This is built for cruise and commercial ships and bringing a yacht alongside its high stone walls undamaged is difficult. In 1999 there were rumours of changes for the better but until they arrive you call the port authority on the VHF, ask for permission to enter and take your chances. Officialdom is found in the nearby cruise ships' duty free shopping shed but if they are checking a cruise ship then yachts take second place and you may spend the entire day waiting. If you have a clear run, the whole procedure will take about an hour. If you have no cash to pay the entry fees the officials will wait while you visit a conveniently located cash machine in the duty free shed.

VHF CHANNELS IN THE CARIBBEAN AND USA

When you are listening to VHF channel 16 in the Caribbean you may hear the curious-sounding demand 'switch channel seven eight alpha' for the USA has its own system of VHF channels and they are not all compatible with the international channels used in Europe. Some VHF sets change between systems at the flick of a switch. If yours is one of these sets then you may find it convenient to switch your VHF set to US channels but if this is not possible or too much trouble do not worry. Using international channels creates few difficulties if you stick to the common channels. There is a good selection.

US VHF channels

Use	Channel
Distress Safety and Calling	16
Intership Safety	6
Coastguard Communications Ship-to-ship or ship-to-coast	22A
Port Operations	1,5,12,14,20,63,65A,66A,73,74,77
Navigational Intership and ship-to-coast	13, 67
Non-Commercial Intership and ship-to-coast	9,68,69,70, 71,72,78A
Commercial Intership and ship-to-coast	1,7A,8,9,10,11,18A,19A,63,67,77,79A,80A,88A
Public Correspondence Ship to Coast Radio Station	24,25,26,27,28,84,85,86,87

The common channels between the International and US systems are:

6,....8,9,10,11,12,13,14,15,16,17,....20,24,25,26,27,28,....61,62,63,64,.....67,68,69,70,71, 73,74,....84,85,86,87

Besides entry fees for yachts and their crew there are charges for navigational aids which can seem steep. When you have filled in the forms and paid your dues then you can leave Deep Water Harbour for the yacht anchorage and bars in Carlisle Bay.

CLEARING OUT

Before you leave you must return to Deep Water Harbour – on foot this time – pay your harbour dues and clear out with customs and immigration. Only then are you free to sail. It takes a morning, but if you arrive at your next port without papers showing that you have cleared out of your last port then there may be trouble. You may have to sail back, and clear out before being allowed to land. This is true for all the Caribbean but some countries enforce the rule more rigorously than others. Some countries such as Venezuela and Cuba insist that you clear in and out of each port you visit in that country and issue a form called a *zarpe* on which you list the ports you plan to visit.

PORTS OF ENTRY

Most islands have one port of entry, or perhaps two. Even though these may not always be convenient for yachts it is not wise to tuck into a quiet yacht anchorage and take the local maxi-taxi (a private bus service using minibuses) to customs and immigration. It is rare for yachts to be boarded for inspection on arrival but you will make officialdom's day if you are economical with the truth when they ask, 'Where is your boat?' Scarborough is the port of entry for Tobago but from Grenada the natural landfall is Man o' War Bay on the north-west coast and a long way from Scarborough. Those who have taken the bus trip to Scarborough to complete their paperwork have been fined when the officials learned that their yacht was not in the harbour outside.

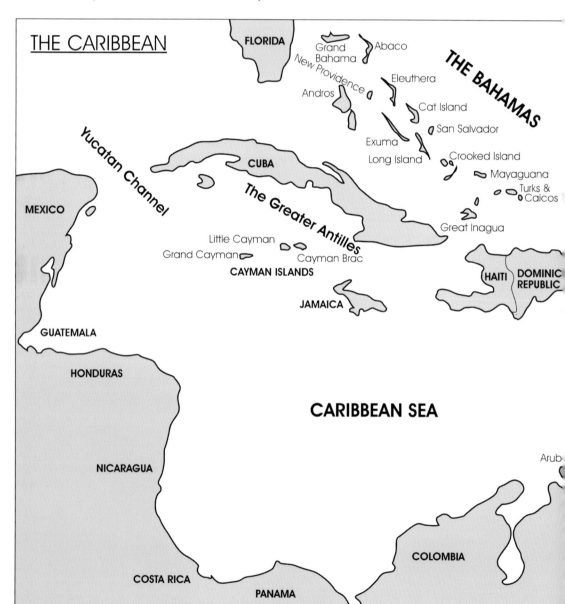

Fig 17 *The main Caribbean islands.*

SIGNING CREW ON AND OFF

If members of your crew are signing onto another vessel, even for a single passage, the skippers of both boats with the crew members involved must report to immigration with the ship's papers and passports and complete the paperwork for signing off one boat and onto another. The procedure is much the same when crew members leave to fly home, except that you must produce evidence, such as an airline ticket, that they are leaving the country. When crew fly out to join you, airport immigration officers often admit them for one day, during which you are expected to take them to the port immigration office, sign them onto the ship's papers and pay an embarkation fee.

MAKING BUREAUCRACY EASY

Moaning about bureaucracy is a popular pastime amongst the cruising community but some streetwise savvy helps you glide through the bureaucratic jungle. Always dress smartly. Or rather, do not turn up unshaven, unclean, barefoot and wearing nothing but a torn T-shirt and dirty, tattered shorts. Officials are not impressed by down-market dress codes. Smile a lot and be prepared to take it easy.

The rules and paperwork for yachts may seem heavy-handed. Every country has their forms and a rota of whom you must visit and the order in which you must see them. In places like Bequia the system runs on conveyor belt lines. Elsewhere, what is expected may be less obvious. If unsure grab the first official you see, explain that you have just arrived and need help and guidance. When you have finished completing one official's forms, ask where to go and who to see next.

Much of the form may be inapplicable to pleasure craft but leaving blank spaces sends you to the back of the queue. I smile, admit my ignorance, and ask for help. Officials have their preferred stock answers to the questions on the forms, but unless you own up to ignorance they assume you know the right form of words even if they are in Spanish. Never take for granted that what has worked once will work twice, for rules, or at least their interpretation by individual officials, change without notice. It is not a good idea to argue with officials but there is a fine line between being obsequious and easy going; insisting on a policy of mutual respect from all parties develops the best relationships.

BOAT DETAILS AND CREW LIST

When you check in with customs and immigration you will be asked to complete forms that will ask for details of your vessel and crew. You can either find the information required by fumbling through the ship's papers and a pile of passports or copy it from a sheet you have prepared earlier.

Sometimes you will be asked for multiple copies of the crew list, and if so, a few photocopied crew lists in your folder helps create the image of helpful efficiency.

Vessel's details

Boat name	
Master's name	
Address	
Owner	
Address	
Details of visit	
Last port of call	
Date of arrival	
Time of arrival	
Purpose of visit	
Date of departure	
Next port of call	
Official details	
Name of vessel	
Flag	
Port of registry	
Official number	
Details of boat	
Type of craft	
Hull material	
LOA	
Beam	
Draft	
Tonnage	
Colour	
Motor	
Horsepower	

Crew list

Boat name	
Master's name	
Address	
Owner	
Address	
Details of crew	
Name	
Position on board	
Date of birth	
Place of birth	
Country of birth	
Country of residence	
Nationality	
Passport number	
Issuing authority	
Date of issue	
Expiry date	

Avoid turning up after 4.00pm otherwise you might have to pay overtime charges. When clearing out in the morning and are asked, 'When are you sailing?' then even if you plan to sail late afternoon the truthful answer is 'As soon as possible.' Any other reply may see you being told to return at a time when you pay overtime charges. Normally you should have 24 hours to sail after you clear out but do not count on it. One yacht in Antigua was given two hours to sail despite the fact that some crew were several miles away in the capital, St Johns, and not due back until evening.

Have your own paperwork organised in a smart folder and include the ship's papers, documents relating to clearing out of your last port, and a passport and immunisation certificates for everyone on board. Several copies of a crew list may be useful. Even if officials insist that you use their forms (they might charge for providing forms) you will have all the information needed without fumbling through a stack of passports. Sometimes they will insist that you complete their forms and still ask for a crew list in triplicate. Do not forget to take your own pen. A boat stamp is not necessary. I have only used *Margo*'s boat stamp once on official business and I am not sure that it would have been appreciated if I had made a habit of producing it.

A ONE-YEAR CIRCUIT

I like Barbados. It shortens the crossing from the Canaries by a day, and visiting Barbados from the islands to the west is a hard slog. It is also a great jumping off point for the other islands.

Where to go depends on the time available. In this part of the world there is a clear distinction between UTC and real time. When I arrived in January 1996 I intended to leave for Europe sometime in April or May. Previously accustomed to my boss grudgingly paroling me for three weeks in the summer, having nearly four months to explore the islands seemed enough time to sail everywhere and see everything. Wrong again.

Colourful markets with a wonderful selection of fresh, exotic fruits and vegetables are one of the pleasures of Caribbean cruising.

I thought Porto Santo's mañana philosophy had surgically removed my sense of haste but it proved to be a gentle introduction to Bajan time, a chronology that places tomorrow in the distant future and regards movement above a quiet amble as a cruel and unusual punishment. It is also infectious. Unless you are prepared to dash from one island to another four months is no time at all.

Choosing where to go is not easy. For a start, there are two Caribbeans. There is the tourist brochure Caribbean and the Caribbean where real folk live. Tourism is big business. The Caribbean is the world's most popular cruise ship destination; there is a growing number of beach resorts; package tourism is growing fast; huge fleets of charter yachts encourage fly and sail holidays and ashore there are any number of attractions and tourist outings. Tourist Caribbean is not a simple backwater but a well developed, sophisticated, international leisure-industry centre.

However, as a blue-water sailor you are free to explore the less commercial islands. Dominica is less than 30 miles from Martinique to the south and Guadeloupe is about the same distance to the north, and three more different islands would be hard to find; Bequia is two hours sail, yet a world away from St Vincent; Grenada is different from Trinidad; and Venezuela, nine miles from Trinidad, is another universe. Islands like Monserrat, Los Testigos or Las Aves are something else again and the outer islands of the Bahamas are a joy.

The locals place us on a social scale somewhere between back-packers and beach bums. Their attempts to persuade us to take a taxi are half-hearted for they know our natural mode of shoreside transport is the maxi-taxi and only desultory efforts are made to sell us T-shirts and other souvenirs for they are aware that space on yachts is as limited as our purse. They accept that for a time we have come to live, not holiday, amongst them and for the most part they welcome us into their Caribbean.

Our yachts give us the ability to escape the beaten track and our sailing lifestyle grants the time to explore the hard-to-reach, out of the way corners that we discover as we meander through the islands and still leave time to savour their pleasures. A lifetime spent cruising the Caribbean scratches the surface of places to go, sights to see, things to do and people to meet.

But some planning is needed. After three weeks at Barbados' Boathouse Bar I ruled out the western Caribbean. Even Venezuela was beyond reach, for once there I would not have the time to follow the winds and currents around the Caribbean. Realistically I had to confine my explorations to the Eastern Caribbean and even then there was not enough time to visit every island.

A favourite trip is to head from Barbados to Trinidad in time for Carnival. Carnival officially starts with J'Ouvert at 4.00am two days before Ash Wednesday. If you do go, make a point of stopping at Tobago on the way for it is a hard slog from Trinidad on the way back. It is best to arrive early in Trinidad because berths, moorings, even space to drop an anchor, become scarce as Carnival approaches. The island fills up to the sound of steel bands and from several miles offshore you discover the true meaning of amplified music. Once you have recovered (nothing quite prepares you for Port of Spain during Carnival) a leisurely passage north takes you through the islands ready to position yourself for the return passage to Europe.

It is usual to make the 90-mile hop from Trinidad to Grenada an overnight passage, arriving off Grenada's south coast just after dawn and dropping into either Prickly Bay or Secret Harbour. After that everything else is an easy day-sail except perhaps the hop from Guadeloupe to Antigua.

You are spoiled for choice. Some boats like to work their way through the islands stopping at those that have historic or cultural links to their European homeland or take in Antigua Week before heading for the Azores. Still others push further along the chain trying to balance gaining northing with losing easting before heading for Europe. The realistic limit is somewhere around St Martin.

If you insist on visiting the Virgins, and why not, then it is unlikely there will be time to make your way slowly up the chain visiting every island. It will be necessary to pick and choose and put in some longer hops. More so if you wish to make your departure from the eastern seaboard of the USA, for you will have to make your way into the Greater Antilles then head for Florida via the Turks and Caicos and the Bahamas. It can be done but it will leave little time for sightseeing and socialising.

THE MULTI-YEAR CIRCUIT

If you decide on a two- or even three- or four-year circuit then for a few months each year the hurricane season gives a clue where not to go. Many insurance companies either refuse cover north of 12° north during the hurricane season or impose additional conditions and costs. In the eastern Caribbean this means between June to November staying on the south coast of Grenada or Trinidad and Tobago. The more adventurous spend the time in Venezuela and points west along the mainland coast.

STAYING IN THE HURRICANE ZONE

If none of these places appeal then, as a rule, forecasts of a hurricane's course and speed of advance are good enough to allow you to run out of harm's way, or seek timely shelter before it strikes. Many boats use this as an argument for staying north and I agree with them, in theory.

The catch is that hurricanes can and do deviate from their forecast track and speed up or slow down just to be sure of catching the unwary and careless. To allow for this it is probably wise to increase the no-go zone between you and any hurricane. At a minimum it should be 200 miles or about two days' sail but you may wish a wider buffer. Either way, during the busier hurricane months when three or four hurricanes blow through, almost all your time will be spent running away or hiding in bug-infested hurricane holes. Neither has any appeal.

HURRICANE HOLES

Most hurricane holes are shallow, landlocked ponds surrounded by mangroves and thick with mosquitoes. The idea is to go in, find a suitable spot, lay out a network of big anchors, reduce windage as much as possible and let the weather do its worst. It may once have been a good idea but nowadays the number of yachts parking in hurricane holes far exceeds their capacity. Before 1995 the lagoon on St Martin was a highly regarded refuge. Then came Hurricane Louis and, depending on whichever tale you hear, either 300 or 600 yachts sank in the lagoon. Five years later Lenny's visit to the island brought a repeat performance.

Hiding in a hurricane hole is not a last minute option. To be sure of a space you must stake your claim early. They do not promise safety from your neighbours. Yachts break loose, they drag, and foul anchor chains in a domino effect until the scene resembles a demolition derby. Cautious cruisers have little difficulty in choosing between this and relaxing in Trinidad before cruising the Venezuelan coast.

CARIBBEAN REFIT

After a year at sea thoughts turn towards a refit. There may have been a time when the Caribbean was a desert for boat services and chandlery but this is no longer true. Like anywhere else, choice is best, and the range of services greatest, in the principal yachting centres but it is a fast-changing scene. Ask around before starting work.

Trinidad is a good spot to choose for refitting. Unless there has been damage or breakages the work is probably not as urgent as might appear. Day-to-day maintenance will have kept on top of many of the tasks that figure in every annual refit. The most pressing item will be antifouling. Every boat collects a fine harvest of weed

Margo *being refitted at Peake's yard, Trinidad, dwarfed by her larger neighbour.*

Your dinghy will collect a fine harvest of weed and barnacles, so it will need regular scraping to keep it clean.

along the waterline with barnacles below it. The low tidal range rules out going alongside and drying out, but the water is pleasantly warm and wearing fins, mask and snorkel, a couple of hours' scraping with an old plastic phone card will soon see an end to barnacles and weed. Antifouling only becomes necessary if paint comes away with the barnacles.

SHOPPING AROUND

There is always someone who tells you that what you want is on the next island at give-away prices. This is probably a good way of route planning but it is useless as a shopping guide. If you cannot find what you want in the local shops then it can be ordered from Europe or the USA. Most chandlers and manufacturers now have websites where products can be checked out and prices compared. If you are bold you can order and pay via the internet.

SHIPPING OUT EQUIPMENT

The cheapest and most reliable method of shipping goods is to have them brought out by a crew member flying out to join you, although they may have difficulty explaining why their hand luggage includes a diesel engine or 60lb anchor. If you rely on your supplier to play shipping agent, insist that they fax or e-mail you their tracking number. Without this, any enquiries you may make will run into a brick wall, especially if they pass the task of delivering your goods onto a third party.

Shipping companies ought to know that packaging should be boldly marked 'ship's stores in transit', a mantra which should see goods safely through customs without paying local taxes or import duty. It does not promise freedom from form filling and extracting your goods from customs can become a drawn-out saga involving fruitless trips to distant airports. It is much easier if you choose to take delivery in a duty free zone such as St Martin. The Venezuelan island of Margarita is no longer duty free and

charges for importing goods there run to about 20% of their value.

Customs may insist that you employ an approved agent to clear goods in, even if they are labelled 'ship's stores in transit'. In some countries procedures are so complex there is no choice but to use an agent. Sometimes the shipping company sees goods through customs as part of their service, otherwise you find your own agent. Some have a fixed charge, a few have a minimum charge and others base their fee on a percentage of the value of the imported goods. Any duty free savings can quickly disappear in fees and shipping charges.

LOST IN TRANSIT

Sometimes when goods are collected from customs they have been opened and items are missing. The chances of recovering missing goods are low to zero because your package has passed through too many hands for the finger to point at any individual. The only way of making good the loss with as little fuss as possible is to insure the goods while they are in transit. Sign only for what you receive and not for what is on the invoice and have this confirmed in writing by the shipper and the customs officer. Report all losses to the police. It will help your insurance claim.

ORDERING GOODS

If the local chandler does not have what you want in stock they might offer to obtain it for you. The key phrase they use is 'We can get that for you in a couple of days.' It sounds heaven: prompt delivery, no shipping charges, and no hassle (to you) with customs. There is an understandable tendency to agree before engaging the brain but before ordering check that you are talking about the same product and that you will be charged the catalogue price. Do not be surprised if they add shipping charges and do not be upset if 'a couple of days' becomes several weeks. Chandlers may wait until their order book fills a shipping container before beginning the journey to you or they may

Depending how keen you are on DIY, it is a good idea to keep one or two power tools on board for repairs and maintenance jobs.

This yachtsman is getting down to some serious welding on his steel hull.

import everything in a weekly or monthly container. If your order has not made this month's container it will arrive next month or, perhaps, the month after that. It is not a good idea to pay in advance.

DEALING WITH CONTRACTORS

If you employ a specialist to work on your boat then before work begins make sure that both you and the contractor are agreed on

the work to be carried out. Check what is included in the price (Are materials extra?), what standard of workmanship is required, when the work is to start and finish and how much it will cost. In an ideal world this information would be in writing but this is not always possible unless you do it. If so, be careful that there are no ambiguities in what you write. For one yacht, a paint job meant to be finished in a week became a tale that kept everyone enthralled for months.

On small jobs it is sensible to pay in full only when the work is completed to your satisfaction. On larger jobs, like having your boat painted, stage payments are fair but a substantial percentage of the total bill should be retained until you are satisfied with the work. If afterwards you have any complaint you may discover that the contractor has already started another job and without the leverage cash brings, scope for redress is limited.

WEST FROM TRINIDAD

After Trinidad, Venezuela and its offshore islands, including Los Testigos, Margarita, Las Aves and Los Roques, are within easy reach and all are outside the hurricane zone. On paper Venezuela ought to be the major all-year-round Caribbean yachting centre. It has 1100 miles of coastline, 80 offshore islands to visit and the Orinoco, South America's third largest river, to explore. It has 32 national parks, 15% of the world's bird species and the Angel Falls, the highest uninterrupted waterfall in the world.

Unfortunately, this is set against a regime of complicated bureaucracy and, even more off-putting, a good risk of being robbed. The threat of crime seems to be greatest along the mainland coast. The offshore islands are generally regarded as no more dangerous than anywhere else. Do not let this discourage you from visiting Venezuela but ask around and check it out before you go.

From the unmissable Los Roques it is an easy sail to the ABC Islands, after which it is necessary to decide whether to return east towards Trinidad, continue west towards Cartagena, Colombia and the San Blas Islands off Panama or to strike north for Cuba and the Bahamas. Heading directly for the Virgins from the ABC Islands is likely to be an uphill struggle but the south coast of the Dominican Republic is well within reach. With the exception of going east these options all involve long (by Caribbean standards) passages of several hundred miles before you can return to your tropical day sailing regime of wandering from island to island.

Retracing your steps west along the Venezuelan coast means going head-to-head not only with the winds but the current. It can be done. Along the mainland coast the winds favour night passages and you may find an east-going counter current but it will be slow, hard work. Once you have recovered in Trinidad it is time to make your way north through the islands.

LATE SEASON HURRICANES

It is unwise to suppose that hurricanes obey the calendar or that as the end of the hurricane season approaches, the likelihood of a hurricane diminishes. Towards the end of November 1999 a tropical wave popped up off the Colombian coast and was soon classified as a tropical depression. Almost instantly it became a tropical storm and was named Lenny. In hours Lenny grew to a category four hurricane. For days it ambled east although every forecaster promised it was about to turn north. Eventually it heeded the forecasters' cries but then it stopped at St Martin, where it spent a couple of days touring the island before heading south and finally disappearing in the Atlantic.

Its winds and storm surge trashed huts on the beach on Bonaire and did damage in the Lesser Antilles as far south as Grenada, which is generally considered safe from hurricanes. Just before Lenny, many boats had left Trinidad, Venezuela and the ABC Islands for the winter season in the Virgins. Sarifundy's bar in Spanish Water, Curaçao, pinned up a list of yachts lost or damaged including one that had left Curaçao and never arrived. Many of the names were familiar. It was heartbreaking reading.

CARIBBEAN BOAT BOYS

Boat boys are everywhere in the Caribbean and, like any service industry, range from the good, through the cunning, to the criminal.

In some places, boat boy trade associations weed out less desirable elements, the best of these offer accreditation to those who complete government-sponsored training programmes and successful graduates normally wear a suitably labelled T-shirt as proof of their approved status.

TYPES OF BOAT BOY

There are two types of boat boy; there are those offering a specific service such as supplying fuel or water or laundry or a water taxi. They have fixed prices and come alongside when called over the local radio net. Then there is the general-purpose boat boy. He is always on the lookout for trade and offers a selection of local craft goods as souvenirs. He will promise to guard your dinghy with his life and claim to have anything you might want – mostly fruit and vegetables. His prices are based on how much he reckons you are willing to pay.

DEALING WITH BOAT BOYS

General-purpose boat boys come alongside, sometimes miles offshore, in all sorts of craft. Some paddle out on old surfboards, or wrecks of dinghies. If it has an engine it is a matter of pride to travel flat out and only stop after coming alongside. They care little for your topsides and unless they are in a clean inflatable, insist that they stand off until you have rigged a wall of fenders. Refusing their services is taken as a challenge to continue offering goods and services until you change your mind. Building on my Cape Verde experience I would give the first boat boy alongside a beer, ask his name and tell him I required nothing just now but if I did need something then I would deal with him and no one but him. Once the word went round I was left in peace. My side of this bargain usually involved spending a few dollars buying some doubtful vegetables or having my dinghy guarded when I went ashore.

DINGHY WATCH SCHEMES

All dinghy watch schemes have a hint of blackmail. Unspoken but hovering on the edge of your mind is the worry that if you don't participate in the scheme, you will return to a missing or shredded dinghy and a commiserating boat boy claiming that if only he had been there it would never have happened. So to be on the safe side, you smile and pay up.

Frequently it is young children offering to keep watch over your dinghy, but giving kids a few dollars for doing nothing may encourage the wrong ideas. If they collect $5 from each of five boats in a day they 'earn' more than their parents. Part of me says that this cannot be good but I do not know the answer to this dilemma.

BEGGARS

I have only noticed beggars in towns and I have yet to work out a satisfactory response. Contrary to what I expected, they do not come in crowds pestering. One or two might bother you but not for long if you ignore them and keep walking. That is one answer, but in countries where the average family income is $100 a week then anyone who can spend a year or more just sailing in a big glossy boat is, relatively, a millionaire and can spare a dime.

One answer is to carry a few small denomination notes in the local currency and hand them out until your daily charity budget has gone. Warnings that giving money to beggars means a close-bosomed friend pestering you for life are not true but if they occupy a regular pitch it is hard to walk by when you have given once.

Handing out a few dollars does more to soothe my conscience than alleviate their problems and it has its drawbacks. I was once severely berated by a Barbadian lady who watched me part with some cash. I was told it was wrong and that my money would be spent on drugs. She ended with the advice, 'You never them give nothing.'

BOAT CRIME

Boat crime comes in a variety of guises and is not restricted to the Caribbean. Boat thieves in Europe tend to visit boats when they are left unattended in yards or on pontoons. In Spain I heard the tale of some fishermen who tried to steal a dinghy left alongside a yacht. In Mindelo there was the story of the Frenchman who pursued dinghy thieves firing a pistol as he went. Until then security had been low on my yachting totem compared to the attention I gave to gear failures, storms and strandings. Yet it is the most likely cause of grief to you, your purse and your vessel. Pay your crime prevention dues before you sail or pay them with interest later.

No one knows the true scale of boat crime. It is worldwide but no law enforcement agency has an overall picture. If they did it would be wrong. Only a fraction of crime (surveys of land-based crime suggest it could be as low as 20%) is reported to the authorities. Since many blue-water cruisers are uninsured, hold only third party cover or are faced with huge deductibles, few claims ever reach the usually well-informed insurance companies. A modest guess gives boat crime a multi-million dollar price tag. Ashore this would prompt vote-winning government initiatives. Afloat, individual yachtsmen are cast adrift to do their best.

REEF CRUISING

The Caribbean is rich in coral. Most islands have their fair share of reefs and those along the coasts of Belize in Central America or Andros in the Bahamas are world class.

REEF LANDFALLS

Coral atolls, reefs and cays are low – barely above sea level – and even if marked by a beacon unlikely to be visible at ranges greater than 8 to 10 miles. Beacons and lighthouses are usually 60–80 feet high, about the same height as a palm tree. Never assume that the first tall feature you see is the beacon you are expecting and that your GPS and charted position agree with each other or with what you see. Your chart may be based on a 19th century lead line survey and the coral will have grown since the chart was last updated.

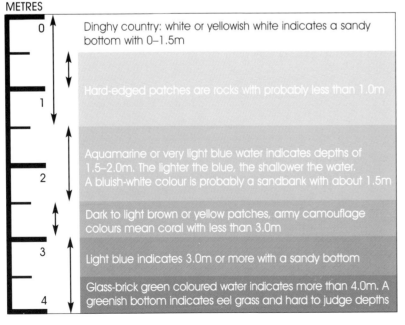

METRES

0 — Dinghy country: white or yellowish white indicates a sandy bottom with 0–1.5m

1 — Hard-edged patches are rocks with probably less than 1.0m

2 — Aquamarine or very light blue water indicates depths of 1.5–2.0m. The lighter the blue, the shallower the water. A bluish-white colour is probably a sandbank with about 1.5m

Dark to light brown or yellow patches, army camouflage colours mean coral with less than 3.0m

3 — Light blue indicates 3.0m or more with a sandy bottom

4 — Glass-brick green coloured water indicates more than 4.0m. A greenish bottom indicates eel grass and hard to judge depths

Fig 18 *Reef sailing: an eyeball colour guide to depth.*

The wildlife in the clear blue waters of the Caribbean are a delight for snorkellers and divers.

If you are not to become a permanent feature on the reef, then landfalls must be made with care and never at night or in poor visibility. You should stand off at a safe distance and monitor your drift by setting the anchor watch function on the GPS to a suitable range and wait for conditions to improve. Reefs can extend some distance from land and it is not good practice to use radar as a substitute for eyeballs. Do not rely on the echosounder to give warning of a reef's approach for depths can change from over 1000 metres to nothing in less than half a mile.

EYES IN THE SKY

It helps if you have some means of quickly scrambling up and down the mast. If you have mast steps make sure they are usable with the mainsail raised and underway. Ratlines can be either of rope lashed across the lower shrouds at suitable intervals or lengths of wood tied to the lower shrouds.

Both work, although rope ratlines cut your feet and wooden ratlines can chafe headsails when you are hard on the wind.

REEF NAVIGATION

When sailing in reef areas it is important to keep the plot up to date, to stay orientated and to correctly identify every feature in sight. In reef country, chart work is nautical map reading and the chart lives in the cockpit where the helmsman can see it. Do not approach beacons for they may be placed some distance in from the edge of the reef and never cut corners, however tempting. Safe reef navigation demands constant, almost pernickety, attention to detail.

When approaching a reef from seaward it will first appear light green with a brown or dark fringe that quickly becomes blue as deeper water is reached. If there is a big swell running, you might see a line of white where the breakers meet the reef, but do not count on it. The light green colour is the shallow sandy area inside the reef. As you come closer this area may be pock-marked by brown coral heads and areas less than 10 metres deep are a greenish blue. The brown fringe is the reef and the blue the deep water outside.

Do not make your approach into the sun. A sparkling sea makes a pretty picture but it is impossible to see the bottom and safe reef navigation relies on being able to see underwater hazards. If you must approach into sun try sailing, under motor if necessary, in a series of tacks which take you across the sun, but best of all is to approach with the sun aft the beam with the bottom clearly visible. Arranging this can determine your timetable for the day. As you approach the reef, a pair of eyes in the ratlines will help you to make out the path through the reef for some distance ahead. Failing that, send a lookout into the bows; single-handers have to make do with jumping up and down on the cockpit coamings. Polarised sunglasses help if only by hiding the panic in your eyes.

Not all gaps or cuts through the reef are obvious. Choose the widest channels and remember that if there is a sea running there may not be enough water in the troughs of waves. When there is tide running it will be strongest in the cut, and wind over tide can throw up sea conditions you thought you had left at home. A slow approach, and a reconnaissance carried out by sailing across the entrance a few times, will help you to decide if conditions are suitable. It is usually possible to approach close to the reef for a decent view. Entering with a following sea can be tricky so keep the stern straight to the seas or you may broach. If in doubt, stay out and look for a well marked, navigable channel; most reefs have at least one.

Once inside the reef leave the eyeballs in the ratlines for they can guide you through coral heads and unexplained patches of dark water. Cloud shadows can be mistaken for coral and sometimes the only way to be sure is to stop and see if the 'coral' head moves. The few navigation marks inside the reef, withies or plastic bottles or the occasional mooring buoy, are usually ambiguous and can be used only with local knowledge.

Although the colour of the bottom is a useful guide to depth, the water can be so clear that judging depth by eye is difficult. Cutting over a coral head may put you aground or the echo-sounder may show 20 metres. Either way it may look exactly the same.

ANCHORING IN CORAL

Never anchor on a coral reef. Damage to coral kills it and will eventually destroy entire ecosystems.

It is usually fairly easy to find a suitable anchorage on a sand or mud bottom if you take the time to do so. In popular areas such as the US Virgins and parts of the Bahamas, moorings have been laid to keep yachts off the coral.

If there are no moorings, try to find an area where you can swing through 360° without fouling a coral head. If this is not possible then lay out a stern anchor so you do not swing. If the chain is trapped under a coral head, it is best to buoy the anchor then dive down to free the lost anchor and chain. If you are anchoring near coral, you must use chain because of the risk of chafe. Make sure you anchor before dark for safety, and dive on the anchor to check it before retiring for the night.

GARBAGE

Waste disposal is a problem throughout the Caribbean. Each island has arrangements (usually a skip placed near dinghy landings) for collecting waste from yachts. If visiting uninhabited islands or remote islands where no such facilities exist then either burn, bury or take your rubbish with you. There are few sadder sights than an empty shoreline littered with the detritus of civilisation. When carrying out maintenance it can be difficult to dispose of oil, batteries, paints and thinners but it must be done safely. Sailing through several miles of drifting garbage in the Windward Passage or finding an otherwise idyllic anchorage blighted by a festering landfill underlines the problems the islands face dealing with litter and makes purists of us all.

10 The Eastward Crossing

Heading home from the Caribbean, the early Spanish navigators learned that the Trades no longer wafted them effortlessly across the ocean, and the benign North Equatorial Current had become the Gulf Stream and acquired a fist of steel inside its velvet glove. The homeward route they developed, la Carrera de Indias, took them from Havana, staying in sight of land through the Keys, along the Florida coast, over to Bermuda and home to Spain via the Azores. It was not their secret for long. Hakluyt published the *Carrera de Indias* in the 16th century.

We follow its variations today. There are four principal starting points from:

- The north of the Lesser Antilles
- The Bahamas
- The east coast of the USA as far north as New York
- The US and Canadian coast north of New York

The first three offer the chance of stopping at Bermuda and the Azores.

TIMINGS

Timing is everything. From the first three starting points there is a narrow weather window before the possibility of meeting a hurricane at sea, and in the run-up to the hurricane season, spring weather in the Bahamas and the north Caribbean is dominated by Northers. Cold air sweeps out from continental USA into the Atlantic as long, cold fronts that stretch from Florida to Bermuda. Ahead of the front are warm trade winds and behind are strong, cold, northerlies. A good Norther reaches gale

force and makes life miserable for everyone. Northers dissipate and the winds gentle as they drop south. Sometimes fronts stall and wait for the next to catch up before continuing south but they rarely make it as far as St Martin. Any yacht leaving the Caribbean when the Northers are blowing is almost certain to meet one or more. From the last, and most northern starting point, bad weather is a near certainty.

In 1493 Columbus headed for home on 16 January. This is too early for decent weather and he was lucky to make it; though to be fair, he made a respectable 34-day passage to the Azores (he had no idea where he was until he landed and asked) and another fast 10-day passage, in more bad weather, took him to Lisbon. He was aiming for Cape St Vincent, an error of 100 miles in nearly 1000 miles of sailing, which doesn't seem bad, given the conditions.

The earliest sensible time to leave for Europe is after the Northers end. This may be mid-April or even early May which leaves no time at all before the hurricane season starts in June. Prudent sailors aim to be in the Azores by the end of June while others hold to the principle that no hurricane dare show its nose before July (even mid-July) and all will be well if you are north of Bermuda by that time.

In 1996 the anchorage in Philipsburg, St Martin, was crowded with boats waiting to sail for Europe, all locked in by what the weatherman called 'unseasonable northerlies'. Days passed; time ran short. At the first sign of a break I sailed and crept into Horta 35 days later. Mike on *Allegro 3* left after me and stopped in Bermuda. As I arrived in Horta he was north of Bermuda and met Tropical

Storm Arthur, which gave him several uncomfortable days lying a-hull.

If you wish to be in the Azores by the end of June, a little arithmetic allows you to pencil in the latest date you can leave the Caribbean and still expect to arrive before the hurricane season. It is 3000 miles to the Azores; at 100 miles a day the latest sailing date is 31 May. Delay a week and your daily average jumps to 130 miles. If you are certain that you can raise and maintain your performance by 30% all is still well, otherwise you are playing 'catch up', with the increased likelihood of encountering seriously bad weather.

FROM THE LESSER ANTILLES

From the Lesser Antilles the first obstacle of an eastward passage is the north-east Trades. These winds, which so recently carried you across the Atlantic, are now an excellent reason for staying in the sun. If you are not stopping at Bermuda then for the first three or four hundred miles you are on a hard close-reach making as much easting as possible in the knowledge that a real sailor would be close hauled. Either way it is several days of slap, bang, wallop and cries of 'Why me?'

I hated it. The squalls that ignored me on the way west paid their respects with interest now. Watching them approach, wrapped in cloaks of dark rain, is like going head-to-head with the school bully. Defeat appears certain but a show of defiance might prevent the inevitable. As a tactic it failed at school and was no more successful in mid-Atlantic. Squalls are miniature gales. The worst approach with a hem of white mist between them and the sea. I think this is spray from rain hitting the sea but it looks like the gateway to the Bermuda Triangle, that twilight zone bounded by Fort Lauderdale, Puerto Rico and Bermuda where ships and men vanish, although this may have more to do with downbursts, sudden 100-knot squalls, than the supernatural.

A swimmer's view of Mintaka *at anchor at St Barts, Lesser Antilles.*

THE HORSE LATITUDES

On this side of the ocean, the Trades and Horse Latitudes are heavy with mystery. Columbus started it by claiming his compass went haywire as he came this way but he was not aware that this is one of the two places on earth where a magnetic compass points to true north. Besides the Bermuda Triangle, it is also home to Atlantis. Plato first mentioned its existence in 360BC when writing *Timaeus* and *Critias*. According to Plato, Solon, an Athenian statesman, met an ancient Egyptian priest who told him of a city state that drowned 8000 years earlier. Plato theorised on the size and layout of Atlantis and its ruling party (all descendants of Poseidon) but without GPS he could only say that it lay west of the Pillars of Hercules. From this has sprung an industrial-sized legend that has placed Atlantis in the Azores, the Aegean, the Sargasso Sea and even the Celtic Shelf off Ireland.

The Sargasso Sea is a sea without a coastline, two million square miles bounded by the Gulf Stream to the west and north, where cold eddies spinning off the Gulf Stream make this one of the most energetic spots of the world's oceans. The Canary Current marks its eastern border and the North Equatorial Current the southern. It is the centre of the great gyre that circles round the North Atlantic and reaching it is uphill sailing all the way. Its waters are about a metre higher than the sea along the Florida coast.

It produces one third of the Atlantic's plankton but lacks the nutrients to attract commercial fishing, for its warm (25°C), clear blue and very salty waters (10% saltier than the salty Gulf Stream) inhibit the upwelling of colder, nutrient-rich water. Instead it is famous for its sargassum weed that provides living space for tiny crabs, shrimp and octopi. Columbus saw it and thought he was near land when he was over the Nares Abyssal

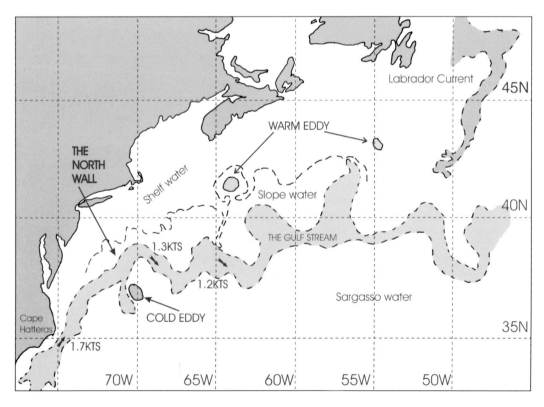

Fig 19 *A Gulf Stream snapshot.*

Plain. Portuguese sailors reckoned the weed (eight species have been identified) looked like the Salgazo grape and poor pronunciation did the rest.

Allied with the uncertain winds of the Horse Latitudes, the erratic swirling current in the Sargasso Sea promises poor progress. Tales of ships being trapped in the weed rank alongside the mysteries of the Bermuda Triangle or Atlantis (do not worry this is impossible) while, under your keel, eels from Europe, the Mediterranean and the Americas have come to mate, spawn and die, leaving their offspring to make the journey home by themselves. That's truly mysterious.

BERMUDA

Juan de Bermudez was the first to see Bermuda when he was sailing home in 1503. The islands soon became an involuntary stopover for galleons running onto its reefs,

making diving now one of the island's most popular tourist attractions. In 1609 Admiral Sir George Somers on *The Sea Venture* carrying supplies for Virginia followed the Spanish example. Somers liked Bermuda so much he stayed. This marked the beginning of British rule and Somer's tale gave Shakespeare the idea for writing *The Tempest*. Today Bermuda is an important tourist and financial centre.

THE AZORES HIGH

Once you have drawn level with Bermuda, the Azores High begins its rule. Tradition parks it on the great circle route between the Caribbean and Europe and yachts heading for the Azores must abandon the direct route before reaching its calms. At first glance, the best option is to sail north to the westerlies and use them to gallop to the Azores. Unfortunately the weather that gave rise to

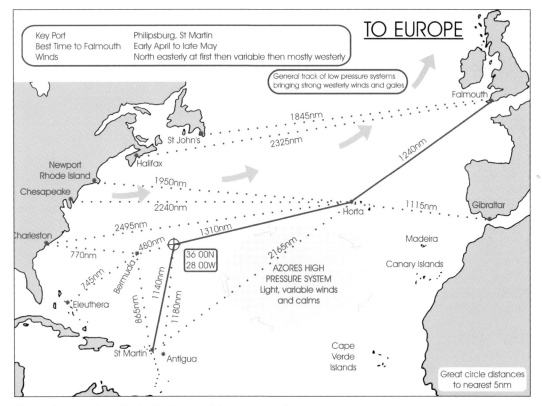

Fig 20 *Passage from St Martin back to Falmouth stopping over at Horta.*

the Northers has moved north. In late May and June one depression after another charges out of the Hudson River to do battle in the Atlantic. Crossing the warm waters of the Gulf Stream drives them berserk and they head east and north, spitting fury as they go.

The art of peaceful passage making from the Caribbean to the Azores depends on finding the gap between the calms of the Azores High to the east and the gales to the north. (See Fig 21.) If you bring it off you can expect a fair proportion of favourable winds. Weather routing is less a matter of altering course to take advantage of today's weather than positioning yourself to be in the right place to benefit from good weather, or avoid bad weather, in two or even three days' time. If you have an SSB receiver, Herb's (Southbound 2) forecasts are useful, for he always looks two or three days ahead.

If time or inclination does not permit sailing, then keep to the great circle route, and start the engine when the wind fails. If deck cargo is any indication this is a popular option. Many yachts leave the Caribbean with their decks stacked with fuel cans and looking like small, overloaded container ships.

FROM THE BAHAMAS

A decision about leaving from the Bahamas need not be made until the last moment, for you pass through the islands on the way to the eastern seaboard of the USA – reached either from the Virgin Islands via the Bahamas or from Cuba. The shortest passage from Cuba is across the Florida Straits but the word is that yachts arriving in the USA directly from Cuba have a hard time clearing in. True or not, most boats take the precaution of visiting the Bahamas. From east Cuba, the favourite route is to swing up through the Ragged Islands and from the west to head for Great Inagua.

The story goes that the name Bahamas is a corruption of the Spanish *baja mar*, which means low sea. It may be wrong but any cruise in the Bahamas means sailing in shallow waters that are a good test of your reef navigation skills. Deep-keeled yachts will be tempted to keep to the (very) deep water passages and hurry through the islands. About 40 of the 7000 islands in the archipelago are inhabited with most of the population crowded on to New Providence

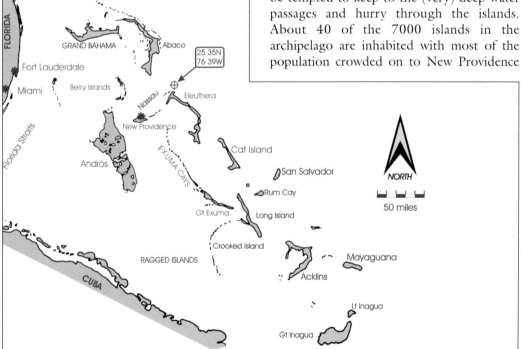

Fig 21 *The Bahamas.*

and Grand Bahama, leaving each of the remaining islands 1500 souls or less. Boats drawing under two metres could spend several months, or years, wandering this maze of tropical islands until they reached the north east of the chain, Cat Island or perhaps Eleuthera or the Abacos, before making for Bermuda.

The drawback to beginning your crossing from the Bahamas is that provisions are expensive and, in the Out Islands (just about everywhere outside of New Providence), limited in choice and quantity. On Rum Cay, one visiting skipper bought up the island's entire stock of cheese and the next supply boat was not due for over a week! Provisioning for a trans-Atlantic crossing could be costly and slow. One answer is to buy all your supplies in the Antilles.

NORTH ALONG THE EASTERN SEABOARD

Most yachts reaching the USA from the Antilles make their landfall between Key Biscayne at Miami and North Palm Beach, after which they move north to a convenient latitude for heading across the Atlantic. How far north to go is a matter of opinion but most would settle for somewhere between Charleston and Chesapeake.

THE OFFSHORE ROUTE

There is a choice of routes north. You can sail directly up the coast hitching a ride on the Gulf Stream or you can take the Intra-coastal Waterway. Both have their drawbacks. Going up the coast requires good weather. The Florida coastline is reminiscent of the Portuguese coast with harbours approached through narrow slots. In Georgia and the Carolinas the shoreline is a bigger version of the Dutch and German North Sea coasts; low, sandy barrier islands protect the land with narrow tidal gaps between islands.

From Florida it is around 420 miles to Charleston. Cape Fear is another 110 miles. Cape Hatteras is 150 miles further north and there are still 115 miles to the entrance of Chesapeake Bay. It adds up to nearly 800 miles of sailing along a coastline that has been eating ships since the 15th century. The story goes that so many ships have been wrecked off Cape Hatteras that their remains create a local magnetic anomaly. *Monitor*, one of the first ironclad warships, sank hereabouts. There are few ports of refuge and it is not a voyage to be undertaken lightly, but should be planned in a series of hops that allows you to duck in and find shelter before bad weather comes.

THE INTRA-COASTAL WATERWAY

The idea of linking the natural inland waterways along this coast began in 1643 when a narrow half-mile long canal was dug to link the Annisquam River and Gloucester Harbour in Massachusetts. This is supposed to be the oldest part of today's ICW. Between 1837 and 1911 the US Congress authorised feasibility studies of different parts of the route and piecemeal work was carried out, but the push to complete a sheltered inshore passage from Florida northwards for small commercial vessels had to wait until 1919 when, direct from their success at the Panama Canal, the US Army corps of Engineers began the work to complete the Intra-coastal Waterway. It was finally finished in 1936.

Starting from Key West in Florida it runs 1139.5 miles north to Norfolk although it is possible to continue to Trenton, New Jersey. However, purists claim this is going beyond the ICW.

It has a nominal depth of 12 feet and is lit so night sailing is possible, but movement is normally confined to daylight hours; for yachts that means 50 to 80 miles a day. Numerous bridges cross it. Fixed bridges with 69 feet vertical clearance have replaced many opening bridges and the remaining bridges mostly open on request, rarely slowing progress. Formerly you warned bridges of your approach with three blasts on the foghorn but nowadays they prefer a call on channel VHF 13 or 9. Some, like the

One of the many opening bridges on the Intra-coastal Waterway.

Bridge of Lions in St Augustine, open to a timetable and if you miss an opening then you are stuck. If you are in a hurry then the twists and turns in Georgia and the Carolinas can halve the distance made good and challenge anyone's sense of direction.

There are marinas beyond number. Details on all marinas are in Skipper Bob's book on Intra-coastal Waterway marinas. Dockage rates vary from 50 cents to $4 a foot plus electricity but members of BoatUS often receive a discount. It is usually possible to anchor (Skipper Bob's *ICW Anchorages* for details) though for the first time since leaving Europe it is necessary to allow for tidal range. This has more than an element of guess work. The tide enters through the barrier islands and rushes through the ever-branching channels as it pleases. Within the same mile it is possible to have the flood with you and against you.

This is 'red right returning' buoyage country, and navigation is from one red or green beacon to the next. Fine, except without warning they change to follow the direction of flood tide and the screeching nag of the echo-sounder is explained by missing a change of buoyage and leaving the channel, which is rarely more than 12 feet (3.6 metres) deep. There is no middle ground. People either like the ICW or hate it.

SAILING FROM THE EASTERN SEABOARD

GULF STREAM

Wherever you leave the eastern seaboard of the USA then the Gulf Stream lies offshore waiting for you. If you think its principal task is to help east-going yachts, think again. There is no such thing as free sea miles.

This is one of the world's strongest currents and part of the North Atlantic Gyre (see Fig 22). On average it moves at between one and three knots but in the Florida Straits it can reach five knots and shift more water every second than all the world's rivers combined.

Along the Florida coast it flows over an ancient coral reef called the Blake Plateau and is closest to land at Palm Beach. Hereabouts it is called the Florida Current, but by the time it has reached north Florida it is veering away from the coast.

The Gulf Stream proper begins at Cape Hatteras where it falls off the Blake Plateau into the open ocean. Rachel Carson, author of *Silent Spring*, called Cape Hatteras the Mason-Dixon Line of the sea with cold water fish to the north and warm water fish to the south. By the time it has reached Chesapeake Bay, cold water from the Labrador Current lies between the Gulf Stream and the coast. By New York, the prevailing winds have moved the surface water of the Gulf Stream far offshore and it has grown around 300 miles wide.

As it moves away from the coast the warm surface water of the Gulf Stream is replaced by an up welling of deeper, colder water. The boundary between these two water masses is the 'north wall'. This is the world's strongest oceanic front, rich in nutrients, heavy winds and big waves. The rapid change in temperature between the cold, inshore slope and shelf water and the warm Gulf Stream causes primed and unstable low pressure systems coming from the USA to explode. These lows, meteorologists call them 'bombs', are most common in winter and early spring. Bomblets in the form of microbursts and downbursts can come any time.

Around the Grand Banks the Stream meets the Labrador Current. This originates in the Arctic Ocean, flows south through the Labrador Sea and into the North Atlantic carrying a diminishing cargo of icebergs as it goes. The mixing process with the Gulf

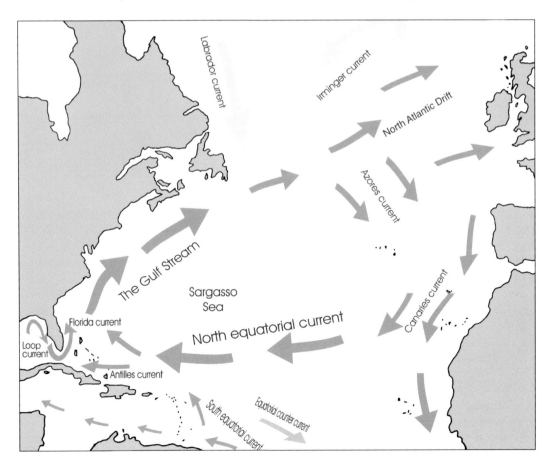

Fig 22 *The North Atlantic Gyre.*

Fig 23 *Low pressure systems coming from the USA, caused by cold inshore waters meeting the warm Gulf Stream, produces sudden downbursts.*

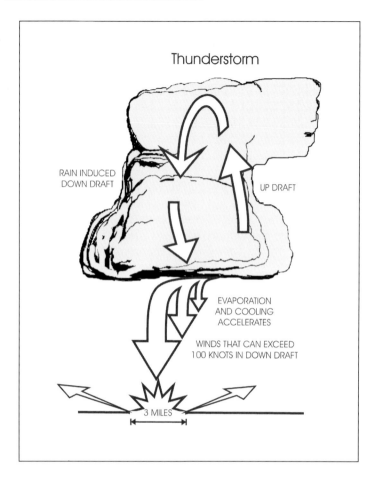

Thunderstorm

RAIN INDUCED
DOWN DRAFT

UP DRAFT

EVAPORATION
AND COOLING
ACCELERATES

WINDS THAT CAN EXCEED
100 KNOTS IN DOWN DRAFT

3 MILES

Stream produces eddies, whirlpools and advection fog, before the south-westerly winds propel the Stream north-east at about five miles a day as the North Atlantic Drift or Current.

As far as the Grand Banks, the Gulf Stream is a distinctive bright blue and very salty. Evaporation of the earth's oceans varies from almost zero in polar areas to a maximum of around 4 metres (13 feet) in the Gulf Stream. As the North Atlantic Drift it loses its colour but retains its salinity.

CHARTING THE GULF STREAM

In 1769 the Board of Customs in Boston reported to the Treasury in London that mail between Falmouth and New York took two weeks longer than letters between London and Rhode Island. The Treasury regarded complaints about the mail as a matter for North America's Deputy Postmaster General, then Benjamin Franklin. He asked his cousin Timothy Folger, a Nantucket whaling captain, who drew a chart of the Gulf Stream. Franklin sent Folger's chart to the Treasury who, if they had ever considered the matter open, now regarded it as closed. After refining Folger's chart from observations taken on transatlantic voyages, Franklin published it but during the American War of Independence it disappeared until a copy turned up in the Bibliothèque Nationale in Paris in 1978.

Nowadays it is possible to obtain daily updates on the Stream along with the latest weather forecasts for planning your passage east. These show not a smooth arc of water advancing steadily across the Atlantic, but something resembling the irregular

TRAVELLING PIGGYBACK

If sailing home sounds like hard work and voyaging in increasingly cold and windy seas has no appeal then you can arrange to ship yourself and your boat home. Dockwise Yacht Transport's (formerly United Yacht Transport) Dutch flagged Super Servant 4 is designed to carry motor and sailing yachts from Europe to the Caribbean and back. In port it behaves like a floating dock to allow the yachts to sail aboard. Water is then pumped out of the vessel's tanks and the yachts are fastened to cradles welded to the deck. Fresh water, electrical and sewage connections are provided to allow the yacht's crew (the limit is one but more might be possible) to live on board. Prices include three meals a day and crossings take about 16 days. The time can be spent refitting your boat. Check Dockwise Yacht Transport's website for details or write to them at 1535 SE 17, Street Causeway, Suite 200, Fort Lauderdale, Fl 33316.

meanderings of a river across a flood plain. Satellite pictures with their false colour images make the Stream look like a Chinese dragon sitting off the eastern seaboard.

USA TO THE AZORES

The Azores lie around 38°N, level with Chesapeake, a couple of degrees south of New York and five degrees north of Charleston. In terms of sea time there is not a huge difference between them and whereabouts on the eastern seaboard you choose to leave will depend on whether you prefer the southern comforts of Charleston over the cosy neighbourliness of Maryland. Once you are out to sea, your route to the Azores is a choice between power sailing and lazy days.

If you wish for comfortable (as opposed to fast) sailing then stay south. How far south is determined by the tracks the gales follow, but in recent years around May most seem to be coming out of Manhattan and travel east for a few days before swinging north. The NOAA High Seas forecast gives their centre pressure and position, adding cheerful snippets of gossip like, winds 35–45 knots, seas 18 to 24 feet (5 to 7 metres) within 300 miles of centre. At least once a day I listened to the forecast, plotted the depressions on a laminated weather map and hatched in no-go areas. Before long I had a fair imitation of the Berlin Wall stretching across the Atlantic and it was clear that, going north of 35°N, before I had made a decent amount of easting, meant hard, rough sailing. Yachts leaving from New York or Chesapeake may wish to drop south in search of comfort.

This line will vary from season to season, possibly from passage to passage in the same season. A degree north or south can mean the difference between fine sailing and a gale. Once at sea the best track to follow can be decided by listening to the weather forecasts. The NOAA High Seas forecasts and Herb – especially Herb – are extremely valuable. NOAA voice forecasts cover only to 38°W. Further east, Herb and regular weatherfaxes are a good combination.

The ideal weather for leaving the eastern seaboard is a high pressure ridge between low pressure systems that lasts long enough to see you safely out of harbour and across the Gulf Stream. If this is not possible then it may be necessary to ride out to the Gulf Stream on the coat-tails of a low pressure system and use the ridge behind to escort you across. Try to avoid being caught near the North Wall in a gale. Each day for a week or more before I sailed, I trudged up to Charleston's Central Library and surfed the web for weather reports. Libraries in the USA offer good Internet access.

It was as Wellington said, 'a close run affair'. I made it safely over the North Wall but failed to clear the Gulf Stream before the next low swept through. For two days *Margo* was pummelled north and then hammered

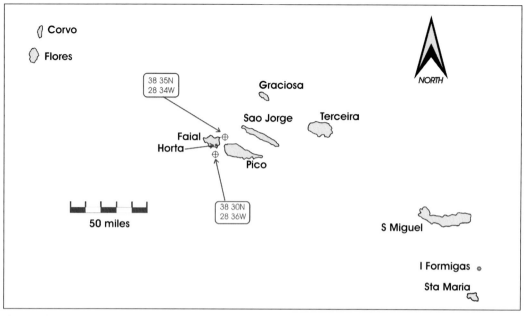

Fig 24 *The Azores.*

south by strong winds and steep seas. At the end of it we were further away from the Azores when the gale arrived. Great.

In 1996 I was north of Bermuda when early one morning I heard a helicopter. I stuck my head out of the hatch and looked around. The horizon was empty. I checked the plot. We were over 1000 miles from land, far beyond the range of any helicopter. Another scan. Helicopter noises filled the sky but the horizon was still empty. Single-handers are famous for having imaginary friends. It was my luck to pick Budgie the Helicopter. I was considering how to treat my unwelcome guest when a dot popped over the horizon and the radar detector went bananas. It was a helicopter from a Dutch warship. Military radars are very powerful. They flew around *Mintaka* and exchanged greetings, telling me that the weather would be fine (they lied) before returning to their ship.

This patch of sea is handy for the USN base at Norfolk and a popular playground with the US Navy and their guests. Manoeuvres, day and night, involving several vessels are common. They occupy great swathes of ocean, fly strange lights and, to civilian eyes, steer unpredictable courses, but their radio chatter makes good listening.

A little further and the seas take on a cold, grey-green tinge as a final reminder that the tropics are far astern. Whales may be seen. Dolphins playing around the boat are great fun but whales have a bad press with small craft. The first whale I met spent most of the morning keeping station a couple of cables off the port beam. From time to time he would surface to blow and, when a wave hit him, the spray he threw up looked like a near miss from a warship's guns.

A few nights later, when I was becalmed, his friends spent a couple of hours swimming round *Mintaka* until my nerve broke and I started the engine and ran away. I am sure that they meant no harm but when something twice as big as your boat swims directly at you, dives, comes up the other side, and all you see is phosphorescence, it is difficult to stay cool. It might be a game to them but a few inches either way would have me swimming. Pumping bleach through the heads is supposed to scare whales away. It might work. On the other hand it might upset them. Whale sightings are common as you approach the Azores.

The tranquil and picturesque marina at Horta, with Pico in the background, is the perfect place to recover for the final leg home.

THE NORTHERN ROUTE

Yachts leaving from the Caribbean, Bahamas or Charleston tend to stop at Bermuda. Yachts sailing from the New York area and dropping south for better weather may find themselves so close that not to stop seems churlish, but yachts sailing on the hard, cold northern route ride the shirt tails of one low pressure system after another until they reach Europe. This is a route open only to the best prepared, most determined yachts. The early part of their passage is over the Grand Banks where the Gulf Stream and the Labrador Current mix and fogs are common. It is also well north of the ice limits for much of the way.

Almost immediately after the *Titanic* tragedy in 1912 the US Navy began its North Atlantic ice patrol to report sightings of icebergs to shipping. Two revenue cutters took over the job in 1913, and in 1914 the first Safety of Life at Sea (SOLAS) conference formally inaugurated the International Ice Patrol which continues to this day to determine the limits of all known ice (LAKI). If you are taking this route do not rely on radar to detect icebergs in poor visibility. The shape of the berg may reflect a weak echo or none at all. In calm weather, bergs may be detected at ranges of 15–20 miles, but bergy bits three metres high may not be detected at ranges over three miles. In rough weather, sea clutter may hide them entirely.

THE AZORES

The most popular landfall is on Faial using a waypoint to the south of the channel between Faial and Pico. If the weather is fine then Ponta do Pico (7713 feet/2351 metres), which overshadows Faial, is picked up over 50 miles away. This is bad for morale for it means that after making your landfall there is the best part of a day's sail to reach it. From seeing one yacht a week boats pop up all over the horizon hurrying for the harbour at Horta and whale watchers and fishing boats come out for the day. Suddenly it is a very crowded ocean. There is no time to relax.

It was rather different when Diego de Senill arrived in 1497. He found no evidence of any early visitors and claimed the islands for Portugal. The nine volcanic islands, seamounts made good, became famous for their flowers, fruit, vegetables, dairy produce and gentle way of life. They are divided into the Eastern Group (Sao Miguel, Santa Maria), the Central Group (Terceira, Graciosa, Sao Jorge, Pico, Faial) and Western Group (Flores, Corvo).

Horta marina is well used to the seasonal crush of visitors and Café Sport accustomed to hungry and thirsty yachtsmen. They run one of the best mail drops around. If you have the opportunity, escape the delights of Horta and take a trip round the island. If the sky is clear, include a visit to the Caldera which once held a lake that mysteriously drained away.

Since 1996 a new hotel has opened and even if the number of flights into the local airport has not increased the aircraft are now bigger. Tourism is growing. Groups of visitors are now given a guided tour of the paintings on the harbour walls. Tradition, encouraged by sellers of paints and brushes, claims it is good luck to paint your boat name on the wall. Some paintings are very colourful, some are those of old friends, but what, I wonder, are the tourists told about the pictures?

LEAVING HORTA

From Horta you can sail for Gibraltar and the Mediterranean, or for Ireland, Wales, the West Coast of Scotland and Scandinavia. Most boats make for the English Channel.

The expected light winds do not always materialise as you leave. A pity, for too soon you are in the cool temperature maritime waters of home. Oilskins, jerseys and thermals are gratefully donned against the wind's menacing chill. For most of the voyage the Bay of Biscay sits to leeward with teeth bared. No wonder the square-riggers hated and feared it. Once blown into its jaws by a gale it would be hard work for them to escape.

Preparations in Horta marina for the return passage to England.

It is traditional for boats to have their names inscribed on the wall of Horta marina.

The seas grow colder and busier. Shipping from all over the world funnels into and explodes out of the English Channel. Once in soundings, the seas are lumpy and fishing boats weave in and out the traffic like small boys crossing a busy motorway. Tides, a nearly forgotten word, draw attention to themselves and underline the lack of an up-to-date almanac. During the crossing the weather closed down and my respect for the old timers rose to new heights. For nearly four days visibility was whatever I imagined. It was only when a vessel came out of the murk that I could guess that it ranged from under a mile to over four. Not once did I see the sky.

It was a hard time, spent mostly in the cockpit drinking coffee, but at least I had the GPS to tell me where I was and what course would steer me clear of the dangers. Picture what it would be like running into the channel in these conditions with your last fix a sun-run-sun plot 300 miles astern, living on a DR and your best guess at what the tide was doing.

I had a brief glimpse of Wolf Rock before it retired into the murk, a miserable, disappointing landfall. The Scillies (I had hoped to see St Agnes), Land's End, and St Michael's Mount were all invisible. I was nearing the Lizard when the VHF warned 'the vessel in position 49°57'N 5°14'W on course 090°T at three knots to be aware that there is an approaching vessel six miles ahead'. It was like lottery numbers coming up. The course, speed and position agreed with my GPS. I was reaching for the microphone to reply when the radio boomed into life and another yacht gave thanks for this information followed almost immediately by another! I tiptoed away very carefully.

I had rounded the Lizard, passed Coverack and was well on the way towards the Manacles when the mist cleared. There were yachts everywhere. The first land I saw for sure was St Anthony's Head. I crept into Falmouth under the coastguard station, turned left and ran up the river to the marina. No one noticed.

11 Swallowing the Anchor

Long ago, in another life, the outward journey to Falmouth on my first Atlantic Circuit in *Mintaka* marked the beginning of a great adventure. Everything was new. The passage round the coast was a voyage threading a route through the doubts, uncertainties, and excitements that beset any new venture. It was like a march through wild but familiar country to base camp before striking out into unknown and uncharted territory. But after my first circuit I had lived the dream. What was left?

Falmouth was not the place that I had left astern. I had changed and its colours were wrong. Where were the bold tropical hues? I looked longingly at the boats gathering for their passage to the sun. They were about to enter the world I was leaving and we had nothing to say to each other. I had barely finished berthing when Ian from *Andromeda*, a Halcyon 27, came alongside. They had left Horta a few days before me and according to their sums I was a few hours overdue. We went to the bar to discuss my late arrival. With that solitary exception, there were no familiar boats from a hundred tropical anchorages.

They were still missing when I arrived in *Margo* four years later. Is there a black hole between the Azores and Falmouth? Wandering the streets I bumped into Mike from *Allegro 3*. Like me, he had been stuck in Philipsburg four years ago waiting for better weather. Now I heard his experiences in tropical storm Arthur first hand. It sounded terrifying and I could only admire the seamanship that brought him safely through. His answer to life after the Atlantic Circuit was to make another and he was outward bound on his third circuit. Then *Bluebottle*

and its crew crept in. We had been crossing paths since Trinidad but as they moored I saw restless looks in their eyes. They would not be staying long. I saw no one else I knew. Was I the only one going home?

Familiar landmarks slid astern as I made my way along the south coast. 'Drop into Chichester and have a pint,' came the friendly siren call but I stopped my ears and declined. Marina life, once so seductive, had lost its charm. I missed the camaraderie of the cruising anchorage. Stopping was no longer fun. How could so many boats be so close together and be so isolated from each other?

But the gods had not finished their fun. In the shallows off Selsey Bill they wrapped a strop round *Margo*'s propeller and jammed the rudder. I could sail but not steer and after an unusually tense few moments I sailed back towards Chichester and was towed into the marina in time to have that pint.

Coming home from my first circuit in *Mintaka* I had spent an evening in the Brighton yacht club bar feeling out of sorts and out of place. Returning to *Mintaka* a bearded figure charged at me out of the dark crying, 'Alastair, I have seen *Mintaka*. Where is the bar?' It was Hans, last seen in English Harbour, Antigua. I softened the news that the bar was shut by mentioning I had some rum. 'Good,' said Hans. 'I have some Coke. We will drink.' We did but it could never happen twice.

This time I gave Brighton a miss. Bill joined me on *Margo* for the last dash up the east coast. Familiar landmarks fell astern. I needed no chart but referred to it constantly. I have not forgotten reassuring my crew that I could find my way up Loch Linnhe in the dark. How was I to know that they had moved the Fort William railway station and built a new road?

As the marina gates closed behind *Margo* it was like stepping back through The Wardrobe, exchanging a wonderland of adventures for reality. For a year or two I had been privileged to be a member of the blue-water cruising tribe. They had welcomed me, helped me, taught me, and protected me from my greater follies.

Now it was over; the world had moved on and I had fallen out of step. It seemed impossible that I had ever been part of the crowded swarming streets. Friends and family had moved on with their lives and it was up to me to catch up. My wife Liz was a bastion of commonsense, a secure anchorage in a unfamiliar world.

At least I did not have to pick up the reins of a job or a business. Those taking a sabbatical must find it strange that their colleagues manage perfectly well without them. Is there still a 'real' job for them to do? Can the job be that important if they can manage without them? Do their colleagues resent their return? What effect will it have on their career? Can anyone who disappears for a year or more be seriously committed to work?

And if coming home means joining the ranks of job hunters, does a year or two as a floating vagabond look good on your CV? Is it a sign of initiative, determination, with the ability to cheerfully accept a real challenge or is it taken as evidence that you are out of touch and past your sell-by date? Is it a sign of a team player or a rebel? Does it brand you as someone who has broken the mould, dared question the orthodox view once and may do so again?

Small facets of everyday life trip me up: new road layouts that everyone else takes for granted, price hikes, the unceasing, repetitive throb of radio and TV news. Who cares? Even the telephone is no longer an instrument for making calls but an all singing, all dancing widget and without a mobile phone I no longer matter. And why do I see telesales people as latter day boat boys barging alongside my life promising me all I could ever want and never need? I think I prefer the boat boys.

Few can emerge unchanged from an Atlantic Circuit. It is an experience that will resonate throughout your life. Be warned, membership of the blue-water cruising tribe is for life and there is the ever present knowledge that all you have to do to reach Narnia once more is steer for The Wardrobe.

Fair winds.
Good sailing.

A Radio Weather Forecasts and Networks

VOICE WEATHER FORECASTS: ATLANTIC AND CARIBBEAN

Time GMT	Station	Frequency	Remarks
0440	USCG Offshore	4426 / 6501 / 8764	
0415	David *Mistine*	4003	Follow by TX on 8104 at approx 0445
0530	USCG High Seas	4426 / 6501 / 8764	
0800	UK Marine Net	14303	
1000	USCG Offshore	4426 / 6501 / 8764	
1130	Radio France International	15300 / 21645	
1130	USCG High Seas	8764 / 13089 / 6501	
1300	USCG from Florida	4363 / 13092 / 22738	
1330	Trans-Atlantic Net	21400	
1600	USCG Offshore	6501 / 8764 / 13089	
1730	USCG High Seas	8764 / 13089 / 17314	
1800	UK Marine Net	14303	Weather at approx 1830
2000	Herb *Southbound 2*	12359 / 8294	
2200	USCG Offshore	6501 / 8764 / 13089	
2300	USCG from Florida	4363 / 13092 / 17242 / 22738	
2330	USCG High Seas	6501 / 8764 / 13089	

NOTES
1 See map for the sea areas used in USCG Offshore broadcasts.
2 USCG High Seas forecast covers the Atlantic north of 3°N and west of 35°W including the Gulf of Mexico and the Caribbean.
3 Radio France International (RFI) is broadcast in French. See map for sea areas used.
4 GEM Radio Network covers most of the Caribbean. In St Martin it is on 107.9KHz FM and its marine weather forecast is at 0700 / 0800 / 0900 / 1200 / 1600 / 1700 / 1800 **local time**. Check its frequencies and times in local papers on other islands.
5 You might get a forecast on Radio Antilles on 930 at 0155 / 0430 / 0630 / 0730 **GMT**.

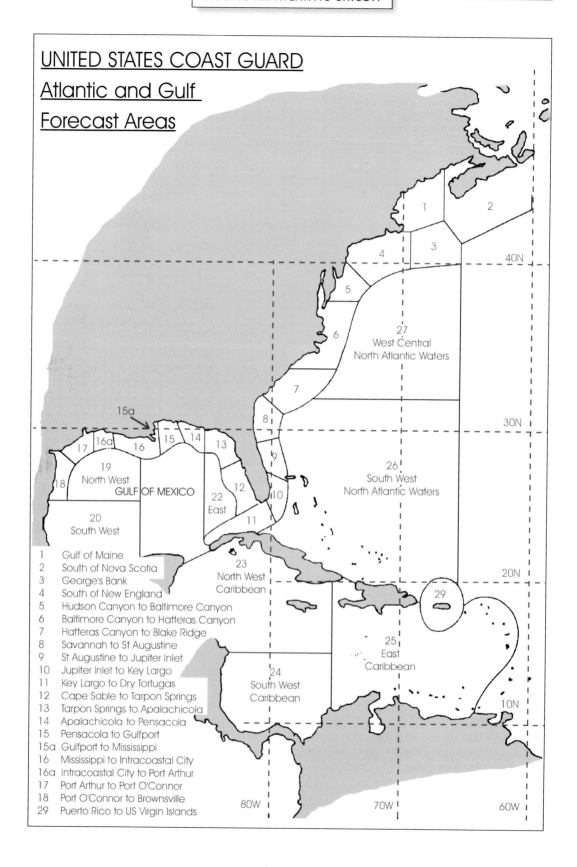

UNITED STATES COAST GUARD
Atlantic and Gulf
Forecast Areas

1   Gulf of Maine
2   South of Nova Scotia
3   George's Bank
4   South of New England
5   Hudson Canyon to Baltimore Canyon
6   Baltimore Canyon to Hatteras Canyon
7   Hatteras Canyon to Blake Ridge
8   Savannah to St Augustine
9   St Augustine to Jupiter Inlet
10   Jupiter Inlet to Key Largo
11   Key Largo to Dry Tortugas
12   Cape Sable to Tarpon Springs
13   Tarpon Springs to Apalachicola
14   Apalachicola to Pensacola
15   Pensacola to Gulfport
15a   Gulfport to Mississippi
16   Mississippi to Intracoastal City
16a   Intracoastal City to Port Arthur
17   Port Arthur to Port O'Connor
18   Port O'Connor to Brownsville
29   Puerto Rico to US Virgin Islands

Map areas (on chart):

19 North West GULF OF MEXICO
20 South West
22 East
23 North West Caribbean
24 South West Caribbean
25 East Caribbean
26 South West North Atlantic Waters
27 West Central North Atlantic Waters

40N, 30N, 20N, 10N
80W, 70W, 60W

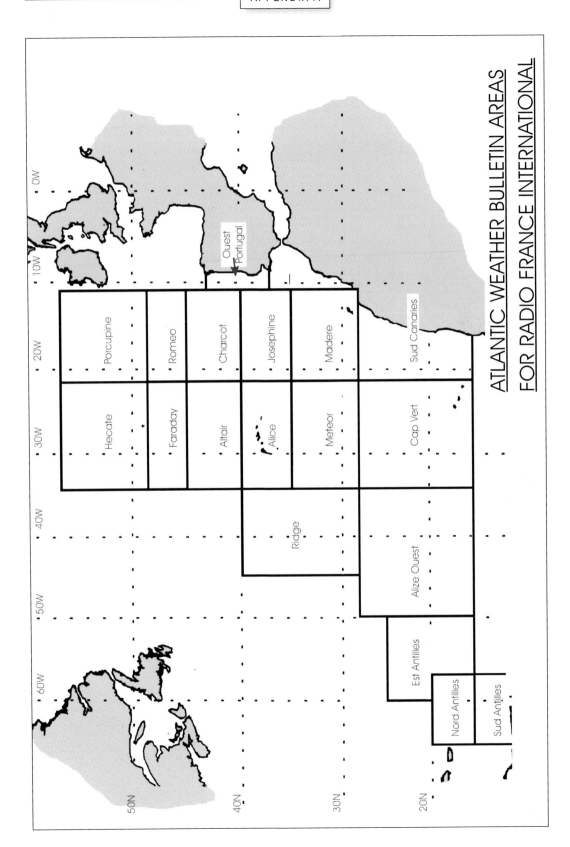

ATLANTIC WEATHER BULLETIN AREAS
FOR RADIO FRANCE INTERNATIONAL

NOAA WEATHER RADIO

In US waters, NOAA Weather Radio transmits local and coastal marine forecasts more or less continuously on seven dedicated VHF channels covering up to 25 miles offshore. Coastal stations include tidal information and real time observations from buoys in their forecasts.

Most VHF radios with US VHF channels can receive NOAA Weather Radio. The channel numbering WX1, WX2 etc often appears on radios but they have no special significance and you may find other numbering schemes.

An audible 1050 Hz tone is broadcast to switch on compatible radios when severe weather is expected in the transmitter coverage area. Coming on stream is *Specific Area Message Encoding* (SAME), which will allow SAME equipped radios to sound an alert when a weather warning is transmitted. If you have a SAME compatible radio, set it to 'all country code' to avoid having to reprogram it as you move up the coast.

Channel Designator	NOAA Weather Radio Frequencies
WX1	162.550 MHz
WX2	162.400 MHz
WX3	162.475 MHz
WX4	162.425 MHz
WX5	162.450 MHz
WX6	162.500 MHz
WX7	162.525 MHz

NOTE

These are 'receive only' channels; you cannot transmit on them.

SOUTHBOUND 2: THE ATLANTIC WEATHER FORECASTER

For some years Herb Hilgenberg, callsign VAX498, has been providing yachtsmen in the Caribbean and Atlantic with individual weather forecasts and weather routing advice. It is a superb service.

He broadcasts each day on 12.359MHz. Vessels begin to check in at 1930 UTC giving their name and position. At 2000 UTC Herb lists those vessels he has heard check-in and, in turn (by sea area, not first come first served), he asks each boat to give their present weather conditions. Herb then gives each vessel their forecast for the next couple of days. It may take some time to reach your sea area.

To receive a forecast from Herb all you have to do is to log in one day at 1930 hours UTC but once you have done so you are expected to maintain daily contact until you have completed your passage. If you can, e-mail him before you set out with details of your trip. His e-mail address is hehilgen @aol.com.

MARITIME RADIO NETS

TIME	ZONE	FREQUENCY	NET
0000	UTC	7.158	Caribbean Net
0230	UTC	14.313	Seafarers' Net – Atlantic
0700	EST	3.692	Bahamas WX Net
0700		14.118	Le Reseau Du Capitaine Net Montreal Time
0700	UTC	14.313	International MM Net for Atlantic, Caribbean & Med
0720	EST	3.696	Bahamas Air & Sea Rescue (BASRA) Net
0745	EST	7.268	Waterway Net
0800	UTC	14.303	UK Maritime Mobile Net
1130	UTC	3.815	Antilles Emergency Weather Net
1230	UTC	8.104	Caribbean Weather
1300	UTC	12.362	Caribbean Weather
1300	UTC	7.268	Waterway Net E Coast of USA & Caribbean
1600	UTC	14.313	US Coast Guard Net for Atlantic & Caribbean
1700	UTC	14.313	International MM Net for Atlantic, Caribbean & Med
1800	UTC	14.303	UK/Caribbean Net
As needed		14.325	Caribbean Hurricane Net
1000	UTC	14.300	German Maritime Mobile Net
1030	EST	14.173	Chesapeake Nautical Net
1030	UTC	14.265	Barbados Cruising Net
1100	UTC	7.230	Caribbean Marine Net
1100	UTC	17.245	North Atlantic Weather ITU Channel 1602
1200	UTC	14.303	UK/Caribbean Net
1215	UTC	8.104	Caribbean Safety and Security Net
1245	UTC	7.268	East Coast Waterway Net
1245	UTC	14.121	Mississauga Net
1300	UTC	21.410	Trans Atlantic Net
1330	UTC	8.107	Panama Canal Connection Net
1400	UTC	8.188	NW Caribbean Cruisers Net
1800	UTC	14.303	UK Maritime Mobile Net
1900	EST	3.968	Chesapeake Bay Nautical Net
2000	UTC	12.359	Atlantic/Caribbean Weather
2130	UTC	14.290	East Coast Waterway Net
2200	UTC	21.410	Central America Net
2215	UTC	6.224	Caribbean Weather

All frequencies are in MHz

B Website Addresses

Chandlery and Charts
www.canadacnet.com
yachtpeople.com
bcp@tidesend.com
www.bluewaterweb.com

Communications
www.radio-portal.org   *ham search engine*
http://pro.wanadoo.fr/radioraft/   *radioraft weatherfax*
http://www.pocketmail.com   *mobile e-mail*
www.jvcomm.de   *jvcomm32 weatherfax*
www.pervisell.com/ham/raft_en.htm   *radioraft weatherfax & buy demodulators*

Cruising Nets
http://pages.prodigy.net/rt234/saili.html   *links to 100s of marine websites*
www.marinawaypoints.com
www.sailnet.com

Distance Learning
www.bbc.co.uk/education   *good learning site*
www.britesparks.com/homesch/   *home schooling for the gifted child*
www.calvertschool.org
www.educationotherwise.org
www.nc.uk.net   *full UK national curriculum*
www.standards.dfee.gov.uk/schemes   *standards & recommended schemes of work*
www.weshome.demon.co.uk/contact.htm   *Worldwide Education Service*

Health
www.bbc.co.uk/health
www.cdc.gov/travel   *Centres for Disease Control*
www.masta.org
www.nhsdirect.nhs.uk

News
www.cnn.com
www.itn.co.uk
www.news.bbc.co.uk

Rallies

epicventures@compuserve.com	*EpicVentures*
mail@worldcruising.com	*World Cruising Club*
www.worldcruising.com	*World Cruising Club*

Sailing Associations

www.bluewater.de	*German Cruising Association English trans*
www.cruising.org.uk	*Cruising Association*
www.geocities.com	*Bluewater Cruising Association*
www.rya.org.uk	*RYA*
www.ssca.org	*Seven Seas Cruising Association*
www.trans-ocean.org	*same as* www.bluewatereweb.com

Travel and Flight Information

http://travel.roughguides.com	
www.cheapflights.com	*no on-line booking but lots of information*
www.fco.gov.uk/travel	*UK Foreign Office*
www.lonelyplanet.com	*supplements travel guides*
www.myownprice.com	*flights matches prices*
www.oanda.com	*foreign currency converter*
www.travel.state.gov/	*US State Dept consular information sheets*
www.washingtonpost.com/wp-srv/travel/ toolbox/airlinecontacts.htm	*airlines and their contact numbers*

Weather

www.marineweather.com
www.meto.govt.uk
www.nemoc.navy.mil/
www.nhc.noaa.gov
www.npc.ncep.noaa.gov

C Spares List

A comprehensive spares package is carried, not for use in harbour when, one way or another, anything needed can be borrowed or bought, but for use at sea where you may need them to carry out repairs or essential maintenance.

The choice of spares carried will depend upon your expertise, type of boat and equipment on board. An electronics expert will carry the tools and spares to tackle the innards of autopilots and radios, a mechanic will probably take enough to build a new engine. A wooden boat will carry caulking cotton, and a steel boat will have welding equipment. Boats with refrigerators, water-makers and petrol generators will need spares for these.

It helps, if as far as possible, you standardise your spares. Having the one model of bilge pump or winch or sticking to one or two sizes of shackle or the same size rope for sheets and halyards reduces the amount of spares you need to carry. Use the following as a starting point to build up your own list.

SPARES LIST

ALTERNATORS
Brushes
Diodes
Drive belts

DINGHY – Inflatable
Patches – in different sizes
Adhesive – watch shelf life
Valves

ELECTRICAL
Battery connectors – for battery terminals
Bulbs for all lights – domestic, deck &
    navigational
Cable ties – various lengths
Co-ax cable – for antennas
Co-ax connectors
Flashlight batteries – for flashlight, radio, etc
Flashlight bulbs
Fluorescent tubes
Fuses/circuit breakers – various ratings
Heavy duty cable
Insulating/electrical tape
Plugs – various to fit sockets
Solder
Terminals – crimp and solder-on types
Wire, various lengths/gauges/colours

ENGINES
Air filters
Drive belts
Fuel filters
Gasket sealant
Gaskets – for everything that needs a gasket
Hoses – plus a long straight length of hose
Impellers
Injectors
Oil filters
Stern gland packing
Thermostat

GAS SUPPLIES
Burners for stove
Hose – enough for the longest run
Thermocouples

GENERAL
Bolts – normal/self-locking – in various sizes
Circlips – in various sizes
Clevis pins – in various sizes
Distilled water
Epoxy filler
Gaffer/duct tape
Glues – wood/epoxy/rubber/neoprene
Lengths of plywood

Locktite – for locking nuts that might vibrate loose
Neoprene self-adhesive tape
Nuts – slot/hex/allen head
Paint brushes
Pop rivets
Rope
Sandpaper
Screws – wood/self-tapping/machine – in various sizes
Seizing wire
Self-amalgamating tape
Shock cord
Split (cotter) pins – to fit clevis pins
Thimbles – plastic/steel
Threaded rod – various sizes and lengths
Washers – various
Wet and dry paper
Whipping twine
Wood – various lengths

HEADS
Gaskets
O-rings
Valves

HULL
Antifouling
GRP repair kit
Paints
Sealants
Varnish
Yacht paint
Zincs

HYDRAULICS
Filter
Fluid
Hose – enough for longest run
Hose fittings

LUBRICANTS
Engine oil
Gearbox oil
Mineral oil
Petroleum jelly (Vaseline)
Silicone spray
Solvents – acetone/white spirit
Thinners
Waterproof grease

PUMPS
Bearings

Gaskets
Hose – various long lengths are useful
Jubilee clips
Seals
Valves

RIG
Blocks
Bottlescrews – to fit spare rigging wire
Bulldog clamps
Halyards – or enough rope to make up new halyards
Norseman terminals
Rigging wire – at least enough to make up the longest stay
Shackles – in various sizes
Sheets – or enough rope to make up new sheets
Winch handles
Winch pawls and spares

SAILS
Length of sail cloth
Needles
Palm
Sail hanks/slides
Sail repair tape
Spare battens – at least two of the longest battens
Spare jib/genoa – desirable if you have one
Spare mainsail – desirable if you have one
Thread
Wax – for the thread

WINDVANE
Spare vane
Spare paddle

TOOLS
Carry enough tools to:
- Do all the maintenance you require in a normal year's cruising and refit.
- Fit all your spares carried.
- Make every repair within your capability.

Make sure that you know how to use the tools you carry. All tools rust so don't carry any that you cannot use or do not need. I found the most useful tools on board were a pair of pliers and a screwdriver.

Most tool lists include bolt croppers for cutting rigging, should you be dismasted. I suspect that bolt croppers man enough to cut rigging wire on most boats would be large, heavy and unwieldy. It might be quicker to use a hacksaw.

D Radar Detectors

For those like me who feel helpless in fog, the CARD 060 Radar Detector or similar devices are a great confidence booster. The CARD was developed by Survival Safety Engineering for the USN; the end of the Cold War encouraged Bob Morse to market a civilian version covering S and X band radars.

A radar detector is easier to install than a VHF radio. When a signal is received, the control unit beeps and the LED display indicates its relative bearing. The stronger, or closer the transmitting radar, the more LEDs light up. This makes it possible to track targets.

Drawing only 0.45 amps the CARD 060 doubles as an auxiliary lookout. With the aerial mounted on the crosstrees I reckoned that it had a 12-mile range. This allowed time to reach the cockpit and watch visitors come up over the horizon.

It earned its keep in four continuous days of poor visibility in the Western Approaches when I learned that it is possible to sort out two or three separate targets. Any more, and its main value is to tell you other vessels are around. This episode finally convinced me that the mast did not shield the aerial from signals.

The CARD 060 Marine Radar Detection System is manufactured by Survival Safety Engineering Inc., 321 Naval Base Road, Norfolk, Virginia 23505 USA
Telephone (804) 480-5508
Fax (804) 480-5683

E Energy Budgets

EQUIPMENT	WATTS	AMPS	HRS USE AT SEA	AMP/HRS AT SEA
Cabin lights: tungsten	10	0.83	2	1.7
Cabin lights: fluorescent	8	0.67	2	1.3
GPS	5	0.42	24	10.0
Log	6	0.50	24	12.0
Wind instrumentation	6	0.50	24	12.0
Masthead tri-colour	25	2.08	12	25.0
Steaming light	25	2.08	0	0.0
Sidelights	25	2.08	0	0.0
SSB receive	1	0.08	3	0.3
VHF receive	1	0.08	24	2.0
VHF transmit	25	2.08	0.1	0.2
Echo-sounder	1	0.08	1	0.1
Stereo system	1	0.08	3	0.3
CARD radar detector	0.45	0.04	24	0.9
TOTALS	**139.5**	**11.6**	**143.1**	**65.7**

Add 20% for inaccuracies and power budget = 78.8

This is the energy budget for normal use at sea.

MARGO'S POWER BUDGET IN HARBOUR

EQUIPMENT	WATTS	AMPS	HRS USE AT ANCHOR	AMP/HRS IN HARBOUR
Cabin lights: tungsten	10	0.83	3	2.5
Cabin lights: fluorescent	8	0.67	3	2.0
GPS	5	0.42	0	0.0
Log	6	0.50	0	0.0
Wind instrumentation	6	0.50	0	0.0
Masthead tri-colour	25	2.08	0	0.0
Steaming light	25	2.08	12	25.0
Sidelights	25	2.08	0	0.0
SSB receive	1	0.08	2	0.2
VHF receive	1	0.08	24	2.0
VHF transmit	25	2.08	0.1	0.2
Echo-sounder	1	0.08	0	0.0
Stereo system	1	0.08	1	0.1
CARD radar detector	0.45	0.04	0	0.0
TOTALS	139.45	11.6	45.1	32.0

Add 20% for inaccuracies and power budget = 35.2

This is the energy budget for normal use in harbour.

MARGO'S POWER MISER BUDGET

EQUIPMENT	WATTS	AMPS	HOURS USE	AMP HOURS	REMARKS
Cabin lights: tungsten	10	0.83	0	0.00	
Cabin lights: fluorescent	8	0.67	1	0.67	Use paraffin lantern
GPS	5	0.42	1	0.42	For noon fix only
Log	6	0.50	0	0.00	
Wind instrumentation	6	0.50	0	0.00	
Masthead tri-colour	25	2.08	5	10.42	Emergency 6W tri-colour = 6AH for 12 hrs use
Steaming light	25	2.08	0	0.00	
Sidelights	25	2.08	0	0.00	
SSB receive	1	0.08	1	0.08	For weather forecasts only
VHF receive	1	0.08	0	0.00	Switch on when other vessel(s) in sight
VHF transmit	25	2.08	0	0.00	
Echo-sounder	1	0.08	0	0.00	
Stereo system	1	0.08	0	0.00	
CARD radar detector	0.45	0.04	24	0.90	
TOTALS	139.45	11.6		12.5	

Add 20% for inaccuracies and power budget = 13.7

This is the energy budget when it is not possible to charge the batteries from the engine alternator.

Bibliography

Note: some of these excellent books are sadly now out of print but copies can be found via book searches from reputable second-hand book dealers. All books listed are published in the UK unless otherwise indicated.

Blue-water advice

117 Days Adrift, Maurice and Maralyn Bailey, Nautical Publishing Company Ltd

All Weather Yachtsman, Peter Haward, Adlard Coles Nautical

Atlantic Crossing Guide 4th Edition, edited by Anne Hammick, Adlard Coles Nautical

Blue Water, Bob and Nancy Griffith, Channel Press

Capable Cruiser, The, Lin and Larry Pardy, Pardy Books, USA

Choosing For Cruising, Bruce Roberts-Goodson, Adlard Coles Nautical

Manual of Heavy Weather Cruising, Jeff Toghill, Adlard Coles Nautical

Single-handed Sailing, Frank Melville, Seafarer Books

Singlehanded Sailing 2nd Edition, Richard Henderson, Adlard Coles Nautical

Travel with Children, Maureen Wheeler, Lonely Planet Publications

Tropical Traveller, The, John Hatt, Penguin

Voyagers Handbook, Beth A Leonard, Adlard Coles Nautical

Your First Atlantic Crossing, Les Weatheritt, Adlard Coles Nautical

Fitting out and maintenance

Big Book of Marine Electronics, Frederick Graves, Seven Seas Press Ltd

Boatowner's Guide to Marine Electronics, Gordon West and Freeman Pittman, International Marine, USA

Boatowner's Mechanical & Electrical Manual, Nigel Calder, Adlard Coles Nautical

Boatowner's Practical & Technical Cruising Manual, Nigel Calder, Adlard Coles Nautical

Canvaswork and Sail Repair, Don Casey, Adlard Coles Nautical

Care and Repair of Sails, The, Jeremy Howard-Williams, Adlard Coles Nautical

Care and Repair of Small Diesel Engines, Chris Thompson, Adlard Coles

Marine Electrical and Electronics Bible, John C Payne, Adlard Coles Nautical

Self-steering Under Sail, Peter Christian Forthman, published by Peter Forthman, Germany

Small Boat Guide to Electronics Afloat, Tim Bartlett, Fernhurst Books

Communications

Marine SSB Operation, Michael J Gale, Fernhurst Books

Foundations of Wireless and Electronics, M G Scroggie, Newnes Technical Books

Navigation

Atlantic Pilot Atlas 3rd Edition, James Clarke, Adlard Coles Nautical

Calculator Afloat, The, Shufelt & Newcommer, Naval Institute Press, USA

Gulf Stream, The, William MacLeish, Hamish Hamilton

Health

ABC of Healthy Travel, E Walker, E Williams and F Raeside, BMJ

Expedition Medicine, B Juel-Jensen, Royal Geographical Society

First Aid at Sea 3rd Edition, Douglas Justins and Colin Berry, Adlard Coles Nautical

Traveller's Health, Richard Darwood, Oxford
   University Press
Your Offshore Doctor, Dr Michael H Beilan,
   Adlard Coles Nautical

Local knowledge

Caribbean, The, Nick, Stanford and Emma
   Hanna, National Geographic Traveller
Caribbean and the Bahamas, The, James
   Henderson, Cadogan
Cuba Handbook, Christopher P Baker, Moon
   Publications
Easy in the Islands, Bob Shacochis, Penguin
   Books, New York
Explorer Caribbean, James Hamlyn, Automobile
   Association
Intra-Coastal Waterway, The, Jan and Bill
   Moeller, Cockpit Cruising Guides
Islands in the Stream, Michael Crator and Gail
   Saunders, University of Georgia Press, USA

General reading

A Fighting Chance, John Ridgway and Chay
   Blyth, Paul Hamlyn Ltd
Alone Across the Atlantic, Francis Chichester,
   George Allen and Unwin
Along the Clipper Way, Francis Chichester,
   Hodder and Stoughton
Alone Against the Atlantic, Gerry Spiess,
   Souvenir Press
Brendan Voyage, The, Tim Severin, Hutchinson
Captain Bligh and Mr Christian, Richard
   Hough, Hutchinson
Challenge of the Atlantic, The, Dag Pike, Patrick
   Stevens

Columbus, James Grant, Sphere Books
Columbus for Gold, God and Glory, John Dyson,
   Simon & Schuster, New York
Come Hell or High Water, Clare Francis, Pelham
   Books
First Crossing, Malcom and Carol McConnel, W
   W Norton & Company, New York
Half Safe, Ben Carlin, Andre Deutsch
I Had to Dare, Tom McClean, Jarrolds Publishers
Lone Voyager, Joseph E Garland, Hutchinson
Maiden Voyage, Tania Aebi, Ballantine Books
My Ship is So Small, Ann Davidson, Peter Davies
   Ltd
Ra Expeditions, The, Thor Heyerdahl, George
   Allen & Unwin
Romantic Challenge, Francis Chichester, Cassell
Sailing Alone Around the World, Captain Joshua
   Slocum, Adlard Coles Nautical
Sailing to Freedom, V Veedam and Carl B Wall,
   Companion Book Club
Shrimpy, Shane Acton, Patrick Stephens
Sir Thomas Lipton Wins, Geoffrey Williams, Peter
   Davis
Strange Voyage of Donald Crowhurst, The,
   Nicholas Tomalin and Ron Hall, Hodder and
   Stoughton
Unsinkable Kilcullen, The, Enda O'Coineen,
   Bodley Head
Voice Across the Sea, Arthur C Clarke, Frederick
   Muller
Voyage of the Nina 2, The, Robert F Marx, Arthur
   Baker Ltd
Voyage of the Petula, The, Frank Evans, Robert
   Hale Ltd
Walkabouts, The, Mike Saunders, Victor Gollancz
When I Put out to Sea, Nicolette Miles Walker,
   Pan Books

Index